BOOKS BY PETER DAVISON

POETRY

The Poems of Peter Davison, 1957–1995	1995
The Great Ledge	1989
Praying Wrong: New and Selected Poems, 1957–1984	1984
Barn Fever and Other Poems	1981
A Voice in the Mountain	1977
Walking the Boundaries: Poems 1957–1974	1974
Dark Houses: For Edward Davison (1970–1898)	1971
Pretending to Be Asleep	1970
The City and the Island	1966
The Breaking of the Day and Other Poems	1964

MEMOIR

Half Remembered: A Personal History	1973
Revised Edition	1991

CRITICISM

The Fading Smile: Poets in Boston, 1955–1960	1994
One of the Dangerous Trades: Essays on the Work and Workings of Poetry	1991

EDITOR

The World of Farley Mowat: A Selection from His Works	1980
Hello, Darkness by L. E. Sissman	1978

THE POEMS OF PETER DAVISON

1957-1995

THE
POEMS
OF
PETER
DAVISON

1957-1995

ALFRED A. KNOPF

New York

1995

THIS IS A BORZOI BOOK
PUBLISHED BY ALFRED A. KNOPF, INC.

The author is grateful to the following periodicals for publishing the following previously unpublished poems:

THE ATLANTIC MONTHLY: *The Unfrocked Governess, "I Hardly Dream of Anyone Who Is Still Alive"*
THE NEW REPUBLIC: *The Narcissists*
PARTISAN REVIEW: *Under the Roof of Memory*
SEWANEE REVIEW: *The Black Aspen*
THE NEW CRITERION: *Mother Church*

Poems from the following previously published books are included in this volume: THE BREAKING OF THE DAY AND OTHER POEMS, copyright © 1958, 1959, 1960, 1961, 1963, 1964, by Peter Davison, published by Yale University Press, THE CITY AND THE ISLAND, copyright © 1964, 1965, 1966 by Peter Davison, published by Atheneum. PRETENDING TO BE ASLEEP, copyright © 1967, 1968, 1969, 1970 by Peter Davison, published by Atheneum, WALKING THE BOUNDARIES, POEMS *1957–1974*, copyright © 1974 by Peter Davison, published by Atheneum. A VOICE IN THE MOUNTAIN, copyright © 1975, 1976, 1977 by Peter Davison, published by Atheneum. BARN FEVER AND OTHER POEMS, copyright © 1978, 1979, 1980, 1981 by Peter Davison, published by Atheneum. PRAYING WRONG: NEW AND SELECTED POEMS 1957–1984, copyright © 1984 by Peter Davison, published by Atheneum. THE GREAT LEDGE, copyright © 1985, 1988, 1989 by Peter Davison, published by Alfred A. Knopf.

Library of Congress Cataloging-in-Publication Data

Davison, Peter.
  [Poems]
  The poems of Peter Davison, 1957–1995.—1st ed.
    p.   cm.
  ISBN 0-679-44180-8
  I. Title.
PS3554.A94A6   1995   95-2670
811'.54—dc20   CIP

Manufactured in the United States of America
First Edition

IN MEMORY OF EDWARD DAVISON, POET,
1898–1970

CONTENTS

THE BREAKING OF THE DAY (1964)

THE CITY AND THE ISLAND *(1966)*

PRETENDING TO BE ASLEEP *(1970)*

WALKING THE BOUNDARIES *(1974)*

A VOICE IN THE MOUNTAIN *(1977)*

BARN FEVER *(1981)*

PRAYING WRONG *(1984)*

THE GREAT LEDGE *(1989)*

HARMONICS *(1994)*

THE BREAKING OF THE DAY
AND OTHER POEMS

(*1964*)

And Jacob was left alone; and there wrestled
a man with him until the breaking of the day.
GENESIS *32:24–30*

FOR E.D. AND IN MEMORY OF R.F.

FOGGED IN

All afternoon the bank
Had pressed on sullenly
Up channel. Quick east winds
Butted against its flank.

It drooped beneath the blue
Like rags hung out to dry.
Sun seared its top, while sea
Supplied it from below.

Yet nightfall in its turn
Gained ground upon the sun.
This morning, under shield
Of darkness, fog has won

And blurs us deaf and blind.
Enshrouded beyond call
We tremble for the end
Of islands, echoes, all.

"TRUE FEELING LEAVES NO MEMORY"

The havoc of your gaze is tidy now;
The slow heat of your shoulder cooled long since.
Yet once the air bristled at the approach
Of so much as your finger to my elbow.
Memory leaves me no more than a flash
Of full moon glinting on unfrozen river.

Along the rolling pathway of my time
I can number the grassblades and forget-me-nots,
Though whole meadows are missing from the calendar.
I touch my finger to distorted roots
And track their features to a severed stump
That stops itself far short of boughs of zero.
What woodsman crept up with his silent saw
To cut this alteration on my landscape?
He finished off with cold purgative fire
To eat the tender wood, the loving leaves
That whispered once against themselves like thighs.

Returning now, I walk through open reaches
Naked to all, where I must once have lain
As warm as a rabbit's beating heart
In a thicket sprinkled with morning, where each leaf
Burned green, hot as a newly-minted coin.

NORTH SHORE

(For Charles Hopkinson)

1. *The Embarkation for Cytherea*

The sun is high. Young Saxons shouldering oars
Trample the shaven lawn. Platoons of girls
In organdied profusion follow them,
Flowers of Boston's bright virginity,
Cool limbs beneath frail garments. At the pier,
Piled high with picnic baskets, cutters ride
The hospitable swell, their halyards eased
Yet eager to spread sail. Across the strait
The islands rise like rain-clouds from the sea.
Here on our hill the house, after its crowded morning,
Will sleep till dusk. Then we expect them home,
Their wine all drunk, their faces gorged with sun,
Guiding their ships, with briny headsails furled,
To quiet moorings.

2. *The Return*

                    Many years have passed.
The house and I still wait for their return.
Shutters keep out the sun, chairs lie in shrouds,
The Chinese vases rattle with dry leaves.
Angry with age, but waiting, I keep watch
High in the eastern wing, my spyglass cocked
To sight the flicker of those homeward sails.
Perhaps they are all dead? I have not heard
A youthful voice for years. When will they come?
The sea still glimmers, empty of islands now.
The lawns are empty. Over the weathered house
Gulls hover, wailing their disdainful cry.
At night the house is silent, and the wind
Steals out each dawn to comb a barren sea.

AT THE SITE OF LAST NIGHT'S FIRE

I scrape char off a board with a dull knife.
Unravelled into dust, black yields to gray,
And eager wood emerges from its mask.
Once it is stripped, the wood glows naked as bone,
Charged with light, suited to hands again.

To comfort this unstrung household, tiles of carbon
Clothed the sweet pine in velvet, muffled all
The liveliness that leaped within the wood
Through post and beam. Is it a fact that fire
Yesterday prowled up the stairs, munched at a floor,
Crumpled a roof, and tempted four upright walls
To tilt themselves into this last embrace?

Within my clothes I shiver at the scars
That overgrow delight and heal away
The marks where bumbling flame has licked my face.

NOT FORGOTTEN

(In memory of N.W.D.)

1. *Watching Her Go*

Drawn by her mumbled entreaties,
We gathered wordlessly around her bed.
She lolled there, shrunken, grizzled,
Garlanded in feeding-tubes, damp with sweat,
Plucking, when she remembered,
At the dressings from the last operation.
Look! Could she have stirred at the touch
Of my hand? Or was it another wave breaking?
The eyes opened. Pain burst at me
As from a cannon's muzzle.
They closed. Flaccid, fumbling
At the unravelled edge of herself,
She died like an otter sliding into a pond.

2. *Dream*

I stood alone at a funeral. It was up to me
To pronounce the oration. My tongue was knotted fast,
And every mourner rolled his maggot eyes.
The reek of greenhouse flowers pressed on ears
Still filled with Handel's "Largo," while the bright box
Gleamed like a conference table proof against speeches.
Toward the rear of the chapel, twisting kleenex,
Sat ranks of visitors, urged to stop in on their way
To another appointment by friends who had assured them
This would not take long. It was taking longer and longer.

Who was dead? It was up to me to remember.
I had ransacked my pockets twice—no memoranda—
And my Oxford Book of Consolations had vanished.
The penguin crowd creaked folding chairs impatiently.
So with nothing at all to say, I did what I did:
Danced a very respectful dance on the coffin.
The guest of honor drummed her cold toes
On the underside of the lid.

7

3. *Reality*

Have I no right to howl—not even now
When the cradle has been empty and cold for years,
The feeding-bottles broken, the rocking-horse rusted,
The christening-spoon bequeathed to hungrier mouths?
Her friends owned her as well: she had nursed so many.
They came together at last, a crowd collected
To watch the last flutter of a fountain, and turned away
As workmen tramped in to pry up the ancient stones.
But they turn away with a sigh: they cannot howl
Simply because they are not frightened enough.
They have lost a landmark, not a birthplace.

4. *Self-Defense*

I came to hold her hand
And sit beside her bed.
Her body was lightly manned:
The siege was in her head.

She counted rags of rage
And wore them while her breath
Grew shallow stage by stage;
Yet persevered in wrath

Against the runaway
Who roused a million cells
To take to their dying day
The habits of cannibals.

Her courage conquered me.
When she asked an end
I yearned to grant her plea,
To serve her like a friend.

Now I can weep no more.
My pain is almost mute.
I did not lock the door.
I did not execute.

8

5. *Aftermath*

The world now has
A gray look to it.
There is much less strangeness
Left in strangers.
Mountains have shrunk,
Trees loom with less shadow,
Even the flavor of fear
Tastes as diluted.

Yet the bloom of your presence
Is absurd as unicorns
Or buttercups at Christmas.
Just as your girlishness
Glanced out daily
From within thickened
Middle-aged flesh,
So does memory
Find you hovering
In a hundred places
Or standing
At the center of the music.

I pray you, do not stray
Farther from us.

WINTER SUNRISE

The crooked shall be made straight, and the rough places plain . . .

Our valley's liquid throat is choked;
Its birches bow, their music halted.
Every valley has been exalted
Under this morning's lavish gift.
Yesterday's whirling storm invoked
Great calm. The snowy land is cloaked
In sunlight for a sacrifice.
The wind has lost its strength to lift
A single crystal from the drift.
The crooked straightens. Harsh hills
Crouch down beneath a roof of ice.

Every valley has been exalted,
Yet winter knows no sure device
To keep rough places in subjection:
With the shrug of a wing a blue jay spills
An avalanche, and lawless wills
Fall out of patience with perfection.

THE KEEPSAKE

What a jewel he had won for his treasury!
A memory thorny as porcupines,
Hard as a gallstone. His bad dream, distilled
From such ingredients as moonshine, lovers' sweat,
And the purr of voices husky with self-deception,
Slept like a tumor—arrested, of course, or no hope
To survive at all. Yet, though the growth lay still
And was hard to remember at the best of times,
It wakened to supply him with a twinge when
He was tired, a bleeding in despair,
A paralysis when prostrate. Could any man
So burdened not cringe with pride, possessor of
So shining, so ineradicable a sorrow?

SPELLS IN SAWYER'S COVE

That was no dream. The shapes
That bared their grinders
And flapped their pinions
Will not be kept inside
The boundaries of sleep.
They must be exorcised
Or lived on even terms with.

Do you recall occasions
When, mid-morning, your feet
Were seized upon by rhythm
You never remembered hearing?
How hard it was to shake off?
How, for a night or two,
Your dreams played you an endless
Game of what, when children,
We played as Fox and Geese—
But with magic at the center
Now, no placid patch of ice?

These paths must be retraced
(Remember?) foot by foot
In rhythm like peristalsis,
As powerful as sun,
The heartbeat of a worship
For centuries forgotten.
Forget? If you forget
Sever the thread that stitches
You to your senses. Here
On islands, among forests,
Tree-darkened, fog-enshrouded,
The dances of our shambling
Ancestors recover
The sources of their being.

The demons and gargoyles
That grimace in your sleep

Are lurking in that forest.
You cannot cast them down.
Now in fog-throttled silence
An idol carved with flint
Out of soapstone crouches central
Summoning you to approach
With offerings of flowers.
"O god of seas and forests
Give virtue to our dances."

DEATH SONG: THE MOMENT

The summer day is kind. A breeze
Surrounds me, as if tenderness
Were its invention. Set at ease
With all my selves, I smile and bless
    These friends: the leathern sage, the mild
    And unambitious aging man,
    The rebel boy, the gifted child.

I bring no trophies from the past
And wish for none. The Deathless Four
I was when young have merged at last.
Time was I wanted nothing more.
    Reduced to one, a single breath,
    The weather breathes me in and out
    Till I shall join with it in death.

Bordered by forest palisade
Whose stiffened hemlocks creak and groan,
A clearing keeps me in its shade
Until I come into my own.
    The waxwing grass has just the hue
    Of glossy hair I loved the most.
    That truth, at least, was not untrue.

I gave away what self I had
To love and loyalty. No doubt
What use they made of it was mad,
But could not self be done without?
    The breezes curry me as though
    Their mind turned on a single breath
    To keep me or to let me go.

The sky is higher now. The sun
Has dwindled to a coin of gold.
I cannot hear the river run.
The forest shade has lost its cold.
  The weather takes my breath away.
  This is the place prepared for me
  Where, without menace or decay,
  The earth will set my body free.

WORDS FOR A SLOW MOVEMENT

A muted smile gives color to her sadness.
Her misty eyes, her tumbled hair are the outer
Permeation from interior tears.

In Tuscany the silver-terraced arrangement
Of olive orchards echoes the hills they have grown from.

What lurks deep in the charcoal hearts of poppies
That the bee avoids when burrowing for pollen?

Under that liquid willow, there in a garden
Laid out in crystal sand, the furrows of rakes' teeth
Skirt the unshaven rock that interrupts them.

A woman murmurs in sleep. Her lover awakes her,
And peril amid the undercurrent of cellos
Quickens the mood of her rising. Like a fountain
That urgent upwelling impels the dancers' embrace.

Gravity sings beneath the graces of beauty.
Look on this picture: under her naked brightness,
Offering her to men like a shell-borne goddess,
Surges as ever the restless inscrutable sea.

JENNY

Jenny takes water seriously,
Strokes its ebb and burrows its rush,
Explores the grotto's twilight hush
Under the silence of the sea.
Jenny takes water seriously.

Jenny hovers on whistling air
In westerlies that laugh aloud.
Balancing upon a cloud
Or wringing sunlight from her hair,
Jenny hovers on whistling air.

Jenny listens while the earth
Shifts its mountains, nurses grain.
Groping with roots beneath the rain,
Sleeplessly alert for birth.
Jenny listens to the earth.

The flickering fire in Jenny's blood
Every morning brighter burns
With flames like crisp uncurling ferns.
Let desire's midsummer flood
Free the fire in Jenny's blood.

LATE SUMMER LOVE SONG

The evening's first cricket
Shrank from your passage
As your feet whispered
Past where he pastured.

Now the sun steals
A last look through the orchard
Where you lie low,
Fragrant in meadow.

Hear my blood welcome you,
Giddy with gratitude
For what shall pass
In the intricate grass.

SUMMER SCHOOL

These tenants of the migratory season
Were children yesterday. Adulterers today,
They settle like thievish cuckoos in such nests
As they can find furnished with a summer vacancy,
And share their sandalled quest of the absolute.

Professor P., expert in semantics,
Teases their drowsy mornings with a lecture;
But once the sun announces afternoon
They strip naked in each laboratory sublet
Among worn counterpanes and last winter's books
To dedicate each fiber of themselves
To the hot discipline of appetite.

Thus in the academy of summer
These scholars, sworn to seek the limits of self,
Enlarge their own by feeding upon others
And learn by process of elimination.
What bones will they have gnawed when they return
To the major business of the autumn
With knitted brows, to read once more of love?

THE PEEPER

No sound—yet my room fills up with thunder.
Behind their windows ladies dance for me,
Heedlessly languid, moist, sumptuous,
Naked as newts. Oh with what zest
Have I applauded wifely treachery,
Lovers in closets, husbands unsuspecting,
Greedy embraces once the door has shut!
Lit by electric light, flesh in a window-frame
Gives pleasure keener than clasping lovers know,
And I make no objection if the shade
Snuffs out the final postures of the act.
Night is my library; day deafens me.
I cringe to hear girls gossip, clatter round corners,
Scold shabby neighbors, squeal at the bus to stop.
Flesh under glass strikes no such dissonance,
Nor troubles touch nor smell nor taste. Away!
        I love at eyes' length!

HUNGER

Western gods are seldom fat:
Priests and painters see to that.
Christian men at grips with Mammon
Show their fealty by their famine.

Smiling Buddhas of the East,
Plump and padded from the feast,
Pensive, wonderful and wise,
Feed the hollow Buddhist's eyes.

Hungering Buddhist solves the test
If he sets his mind at rest
By the Way that Buddha set him:
"You, who love your god, forget him."

Yet, in matters Eucharistic,
Westerner is proved the mystic:
Though the mystery defeats him,
If he loves his God, he eats Him.

PERIPHERAL VISION

The corner of the eye
Is where my visions lie.
A startle, or a slant
From squirrel, bird or plant,
Turns hard and fast if seen
By eyes asquint and keen.

Rather the shape and style
That only just beguile
The tail-end of my sight
Than organizing light
To tidy up the view
And clear it out of true.

THE FIRSTLING

Down the soft hillside
The farm girl came frolicking,
Rosy and ribald and
Looking for company.

Quick by a willow she
Stripped for the cooling brook.
Over her bursting breasts
Water meandered.

Soon she lolled ripe for the
Fumble of fingers, the
Plunging of pulses, the
Lovely unstringing,

But shortly, unhandled, she
Mounts up the hill again,
Carrying news
To set loose in the village.

How many summers had
Man and boy come to strive
With the nymph naked,
And all been rewarded—

All but this firstling, who,
Shirking his trial, lies
Dry-mouthed and still
Beneath the charmed hill?

SACRIFICIAL MASK

Mirror, Mirror on the wall,
Who is falsest of us all?

Only silence. Does this mask
Hear no questions mirrors ask?

I have modelled every crease
To ensure the people's peace

Who go easy when they see
Kindly love encasing me.

Now the eyes behind the face
Blink their horror and disgrace.

They know well what price was paid
For the features I have made.

FOOT

Alert, remote, my foot
Engages with the floor
Because it is so ordered.

The voices of control
Convey their miracle.
Ten inches and five feet

Of distance, more or less,
Divide my top and toe;
And yet I flex my foot

For leaping or for lagging
By twisting with the toes
Or angling with the ankle,

Contracting at the instep
Or stretching out the tendon,
By stamping, stopping.

My orders reach their man.
But what when mind, crippled
And faltering in stride,
Casts off and staggers footloose?

THE STAR WATCHER

(For R. F.)

Stars had the look of dogs to him sometimes,
Sometimes of bears and more than once of flowers,
But stars were never strange to him because
Of where they stood. We knew him jealous
And in his younger days a little sly
About his place among the poesies;
Yet when his eyes showed envy or delight
They rested upon knowledge, not on distance.
All that he saw, up close or farther off,
Was capable of being understood,
Though not by him perhaps. He had enough
Of science in him to be optimistic,
Enough of tragedy to know the worst,
Enough of wit to keep on listening,
Or watching, when it came to stars. He knew,
Across the distance that their light might travel,
That nothing matters to the stars but matter,
Yet that their watchers have to learn the difference
Between the facts of knowledge and of love,
Or of love's opposite, which might be hate.
Therefore he taught, and, like the best of teachers,
Often annoyed the students at his feet,
Whether they learned too much or not enough,
Whether or not they understood him wrong.
Two was his pleasure, and the balance held
In love, in conversation, or in verse.
With knuckles like burled hemlock roots, his hands
Had, in his age, smooth palms as white as milk;
And, through the massy cloudbanks of his brows,
His eyes burned shrewdly as emerging stars.

TO A MAD FRIEND

I may look fine at the moment, but like you
I have capered and somersaulted in the street,
While, hoisted upon my shoulders, someone's face
Smiled at my friends and answered the telephone;
Or hovered, like a fish with nose against
A rock, in elements I could not breathe.
You've seen us in every land you've travelled through:
Our ties were tied, our shoes were always shined,
But icy eyes and tightness around the smile
Are marks enough to know your brothers by.
Rest easier, friend: we've all walked through your dreams
And are no strangers to that company.

FINALE: PRESTO

"I think I'm going to die," I tried to say.
My husband, standing over the bed, labored
To hear words in the sounds as they emerged.
He shook his head as briskly as a dog
Taking its first steps on land, and acted deaf
To the words he knew he might have heard me speak.
Throughout this evil month I've said the same
To every visitor. It comes out gibberish.
The night nurse, hiding in my room to smoke,
My daughter, prattling anxiously of clothes,
My son, weary from four hundred miles
Of travel every weekend—all escape
By smiling, talking, plumping up my pillows.
I wrack myself to utter any word;
They reply, "Dear, I cannot understand you."
If I could move this hand, this leg, I'd write
Or stamp a fury on the sterile floor.
I'd act the eagle. I, who winced at death
If the neighbor's second cousin passed at ninety,
Who bore an ounce of pain so awkwardly
It might have been a ton, who fed myself
With visions of good order in a future
Near enough to reach for—I am cumbered
With armlessness, with leglessness, with silence.
To say the word so anyone could hear it!
Death, do you hear me, death? The room is empty.
Only the one word now, hearers or no.
I batter at it with convulsive shouts
That resonate like lead. Again. And now—
Listen—it rings out like a miracle.
No one stands near. The corridor is dark.
"Death." I sing the lovely word again,
And footsteps start to chatter down the hall
Towards my bed. Smiling at every sound,
I see that no one can arrive in time,
And I, emptying like water from a jug,
Will be poured out before a hand can right me.
That word raised echoes of a halleluia.
Death, do you hear me singing in your key?

WREN

The dark wood moved.
Between the stumps
Along the brook
Life lingered, danced.

Leaves out of place?
Wind at a twig?
The shadow delayed,
Flickered, advanced.

By the fringe of a thirsty
Thicket, the thing
Flirted its flag
Of a tail and pranced

Till a stray sunbeam
Discovered its eye.
The needle beak
Froze fixed, entranced.

Though signs of wren
Forsook the scene,
Through circumstance
The wood had danced.

GOODBYE

A sailing cloud of pipe smoke wrecked itself
Against the wall. He watched its noiseless crash
And waited among the memories of the room
For the expected footstep on the stair.
Last meeting. What would be said he knew,
Had known for months. The words had turned to stone
And now were to be quarried, shaped, laid in place,
Wrenched from where they had rested all this time.
A rattle at the door downstairs, the sound
Of feet ascending, steps with a slump in them,
As though the climber's bones had turned to chalk.
Then for the hundredth time, the handle turned,
The door opened before her, she came in.
Her smile gleamed out as she took off her coat,
And his eyes drank deep, thirst even now unquenched
For hair as tawny as a winter hillside,
Eyes blue and vague, hands with a milkmaid's grip,
Legs strong for walking. Beneath her clothes he could
Remember breast and belly soft as fruit—
Yet slack for him. Fruit never gave itself
Less eagerly to a hungry mouth than she did.

"Well." With another smile she took her seat,
Shook out her hair, waited as usual.
Her cigarette filled silence till he spoke.
"You came . . . We had to talk . . . It's time . . . You know?"
"Yes," she said rapidly, "I guess it is."
He'd spoken it all before—the give and take
Of weary argument, nothing to win or lose—
But now, with a growing chill, he knew his mind
Because her true indifference had come through.
All he had wanted was to win a debate,
Persuade her against her will she wanted him,
Make her admit it even though she lied.
The silence fell like snowflakes, and the swirl
Grew thicker, stronger, deeper. In his head
A frightened hammering began. This wasn't the way

He had expected it to be at all!
She wasn't there; she simply was not interested.
No argument—she did not care to argue.
Yet she was kind, and in her kindness waited
Till he should let her go. He came and tried
To touch her, touch her with his hands, since words
Had lost their power with her. But her flesh
Was hearkening to something else. He felt
He could shriek at her, and still she would be deaf;
Could strike her, and her body feel no blow.

Yet she was crying, staring straight ahead.
He knew the tears were not for him. "All right,"
He said, "I'm sorry this is how it ends,
But there's no point going on," knowing that he
Had to pretend to take the final step
Although they both knew it was long since taken.

A kiss upon the cheek, as for an older brother,
And she was gone. Her steps went slowly down
One flight, then headlong down a second, like
A bird who finds the door of its cage left open.
The street door slammed behind her, and he heard
The sound of it for hours, it seemed, because
The clang of hammers started in his head
Again, and now he knew they would not stop.

THE WINNER

I hear a child inside,
Crying to be let out.

"No," shouts the swaggering Self,
"Mind shall destroy all doubt.
Out with all doubt I say!
Stifle that treacherous word!
I have high deeds to do
Twirling my deathly sword."

Mind's on his mettle now,
Deft at his surgical art,
Stunning my pain with pain,
Drowning the infant heart.

THE DEATH OF THE VIRGIN (*Rembrandt*)

Our ears were barren to the rising music:
We waited with the smell of clammy sweat,
With her blue hands twitching at the sheet,
With the grating of spent lungs. Strain as we might
To tear our sight from the face of the drowning woman
(Flopped on the white bed anyhow), our eyes were blind
To the swirl of angels coursing heavenward
With news of an acquisition for the Kingdom—
The soul of one who, spotless from her conception,
Came to that company peerless and deserved
The loudest, most triumphant kind of announcement.
For those of us still crouched around the bed
There was no news except the end of breath,
The end of motion, the repose of will.
The wasted part of her was left to us.

ARTEMIS

See how this girl, trim,
Fragile as porcelain,
Poises within herself,
Standing apart with hounds.

Chaste in her garments, loins
Crisp as a boy's, her knees
Rigid as spear-shafts,
She stares down a victim,

Lowers her eyelids,
Lets the white linen fall,
Stretches, as unaware
Of the blood rising,

Curls like a kitten,
Unclenches her fingers,
While her demented eyes
Flutter in hiding.

Now, when the hunt is closed
Hard on the quarry,
Savage in chase at last,
"Die!" she screams, riding.

THE SUICIDE

Poor starling. Her cry was sharp enough to draw blood
As she braced her whistling head and squeezed her feet
Clamp upon her local chimney top
And glared as hard as the sky that looked her down.
Taut-muscled on the ground, she pecked and pecked
Whatever she scratched up, never sure
Which grains were food, which grains were only gravel.
Just so her loves, random as a vine.
Curse those who kept her food from her until
She'd learnt their tricks! Her hungry eyes became
Their sentinels, on watch for where the heart
Lurked, to have it out and peck peck peck—
And yet her beak most often fell on bone
Until the day she turned it on herself
And dizzyingly sang, within her throat
The sigh of the slain, the grunt of the executioner.

THE BREAKING OF THE DAY

(Genesis 32:24-30)

1.   *The Birthright*

A half-and-half affair, I grew from the union
Of a buxom, vital, Titian-haired New Yorker
And the cockerel moodiness of a Tyneside orphan.
She, in the gabble of Upper-West-Side tea dances,
Looked feverish when her father, the cotton merchant,
Stumped off to synagogue to pray for his brothers' funerals.
Later, she chose not to explain to me the difference
Between the Talmud and the Pentateuch,
And I, unlearned in the ways of Shabbas and Seder,
Had to read them up later in the works of Wouk.
Not until I got to be thirteen
Did it cross my mind I might be half a Jew,
And not until an angry schoolmate told me:
I heard the malice rising in his voice.

To take a step backward, look once more at my father,
Who rarely saw a Jew till he was twenty.
Sweet-voiced, he was made much of by the Rector
As he raised his boy soprano at St. Simon's
And learned his Apostles' Creed and Catechism.
For him a Jewess was rich with secret knowledge
And raven-haired—he'd read Scott and Disraeli.
Jews, on the other hand, were money-lenders.

When the schoolboy told me of my being Jewish
I asked my parents, Was he telling truth?
My mother said that they had *meant* to tell me.
My father said it didn't really matter
Because I was Anglican by half.
The question I had asked was left unanswered,
And all the knowledge that I got for asking
Was learning that they had no wish to answer
And that my question led to other questions.

2. *The Wrestler*

Fastened by the skewer of despair in a hotel room,
Steeling under anger and lust, the leers of the sergeants,
Bound hand and foot on a tufted counterpane,
I lay in prison while the night air hardened.
God burst in at last with the cry of a prairie rooster,
And in the dawn my heart began again.
My limbs were kindled with a course of blood,
And I shot from my cell into the sunrise streets
To trudge for miles while I turned a new weight in my hands:
Cherished sin, to carry for my burden—
Mine for my charge, my signal, my evermore mark,
That a single touch had bestowed, and not of my choosing.

After sunrise came the shock of daylight:
To grapple with my sinfulness I must
Put God in words. The only words I knew
Were those that God had spoken in his books,
The books that England had prepared for Him.

3. *The Gift of Tongues*

God my father spoke in the calm of evening.
He spoke in iambs beating in the darkness.
His pipe glowed and its vapor blossomed upward.
The child at his feet drank in the heady honey
Of his voice, his presence, his attention
While the elm-leaves rustled their assent.
The words he spoke—from Oreb or from Sinai—
Were, had I known it, many times outworn
Except for those that burned as his alone:

> *I shall come back to die*
> *From a far place at last,*
> *After my life's carouse*
> *In the old bed to lie*
> *Remembering the past*
> *In this dark house.*

His voice wore all the costumes of our tongue,
And in the dark I trembled at the golden
Din of the past resounding in my ears.
These were the words that God had always spoken,
As, "This is my beloved Son, in whom
I am well pleased." The words belonged to him,
And now, as their custodian, he gave
His hoard to me at night beneath the trees.
I counted them for years before I learned
The spending of them; yet I did not know
That he had given them away for good
And that from that night forward he would walk
The earth like any natural man,
His powers incomplete, his magic gone.

4. *The Salt Land*

After baptisms, confessions, confirmations,
Communions by the dozen, rites and choirs,
Cranmer's great book was absorbed into my bloodstream,
And all the words turned into words again.
The fish died while I stood before the Cross:
Christ's blood, they said, was infinitely precious,
But all I knew of it was that they said so.

Later still I watched my mother's mother
(She wept because she must outlive her daughter)
Being interred at a non-religious funeral
With a eulogy delivered by her doctor
At a Lexington Avenue mortician's chapel.
This was the end. The Jewesses were dead.
My female life-line was extinguished.

5. *The Dead Sea*

The womb that held me in its lake is dry,
The bounty parched and powdered. He that held
A weapon or a scepter or a cross
Has lost the good of his grasp and sits in silence,
Who took it on himself to shake the earth.
You, mother, rocked me bloodless in my cradle
And yearned to free me from my ancestors:
The womb of the Goddess denied she had been born.

So both were outcasts from their ancestry.
No offerings for them, no worshippers—
Except for me, who worshipped in myself
Crude copies of their skilled originals,
To find at last, on the baked earth of this shrine,
That I am no more Christian, no more Jew.

The afternoon is dark and not with rain.

6. *Delphi*

The crackle of parched grass bent by wind
Is the only music in the grove
Except the gush of the Pierian Spring.
Eagles are often seen, but through a glass
Their naked necks declare them to be vultures.
The place is sacred with a sanctity
Now faded, like a kerchief washed too often.
There lies the crevice where the priestesses
Hid in the crypt and drugged themselves and spoke
Until in later years the ruling powers
Bribed them to prophesy what was desired.
Till then the Greeks took pride in hopelessness
And, though they sometimes wrestled with their gods,
They never won a blessing or a name
But only knowledge.
                             I shall never know myself
Enough to know what things I half believe
And, half believing, only half deny.

THE CITY AND THE ISLAND

(*1966*)

EVERY WORD FOR J.T.D. TO KEEP

TRAVELLING AMONG ISLANDS

(For Alastair Reid)

Alone, alone but not without resources
Even in his melancholy smile,
He keeps as property no more than a razor
And a laundered shirt to take him through tomorrow.
Clean as a cat he sits, nibbling his fingers
To make himself still cleaner, tooth and nail.

Love he knows in plenty—all the love
A sailor finds in port, with every girl flowery—
But he loves them dearly as they wave goodbye,
And all his friendships are perfect in chance meetings.
Departing, he leaves others to remember
And moves toward another destination
Where faces will wash clean again to see him.

Only the sea is home to him.
He is nourished by land as others are by water.
He lives on less than would supply a lifeboat
And his lovers lie in wait among the islands—
Circe, Penelope. Nausicaa, Calypso.

LETTER FROM A CITY DWELLER

Only from islands can you shape the city,
Plumes bobbing from a hundred miles away.
Towers like tusks jut out from the horizon.
It makes a handsome profile, from a distance.

Invisible of course from islands are
The cells and walk-ups that we use for hiding,
Nor can you hear the language of the streets.
The city has would-be islands of its own:

Neighborhoods—the few that still remain—
Cliques and clubs, gangs and offices,
All the niches where an anyone
Can lose himself and find himself at once.

Such camouflage is hard to achieve on islands.
Your trouble is that there you always know
Exactly where you are. The sea and land
Leave you no ambiguities on that score.

Islands provide no place to hide
From him or her or them or from yourself.
They offer you exposure to the sky
And silence, to the wind and stinging rain,

Even to fellow-men. While you can watch
The city from a distance, our shivering city
Has set so many walls up for protection
That islands are less visible than ever,

And fewer islanders stay home to vote
Every election. Not so our citizens,
Who multiply like pages being printed
Without a binding or conclusion.

Yet even though we lead a sheltered life
We have advantages unknown to you:
We pick and choose: we never meet the poor
And can with ease ignore their poor existence.

We have built barricades against the cold
Of weather and of hearts: for we believe
That there is really such a thing as comfort,
That it can be possessed as well as given.

Islands offer aspirants a chance
To learn what can be learned from nakedness,
Since there clothes serve exclusively for weather
And not as one more form of hiding place.

The danger on your islands is that you
Can grow so giddy as to think the sea
Will always be content to be your servant
And that your selves, astride their tiny kingdom,

Can shake their fists at all that lies onshore.
Sainthood is perfect training for an island,
As islands are for sainthood. So it was
With John, enraged in his cave on Patmos.

He beat his breast until the walls resounded,
And answered in his Book. At intervals
He peered from the cave's mouth, downhill to the harbor,
Where shipping came and moored, unmoored and went.

Angry each time, he turned back to the cave
Where the Great Beast crouched, hideous and waiting.
Such enterprise is suited to an island
If that's the work you like. I wish you luck.

But keep in mind, winter is cold offshore.
We're glad to see you when you're passing through.
When you haven't caught sight of a smile in ages,
Don't hesitate. Take passage for the city.

SONG: BRIGHT BEING

Past the rich meadowland of the senses
Shade mingles and stirs in the clearings.
In that island where oranges blossom
    I seek you, child, again.

On the shore where surf scurries hissing
And the sand scrapes under your shoulder,
Where tides nuzzle sweetly together,
    I hold you, child, again.

In the heat of wet tongues and embraces,
In the shuddering bed where Love
Can never quite be requited,
    I lie with you again.

That childhood has lasted forever
In a forest of tottering archways.
Sink down in the echoing moonlight
    And die with me again.

THE EMIGRATION: NEWFOUNDLAND 1965

Love, there are reasons why I must be free
        To put to sea.
    No matter how the body aches
To keep in touch, touch has its failures too.
The mind is helped to heal by travelling,
      And so I offer to the wake's
        Brutal unravelling
The old perplexities of course and crew.

My dream has never changed: abandoned far
      From shore I float
    Aboard an ill-found boat
Unhelped by oar or sail, landfall or star
To guide by. Currents jostle me at will.
      The wallowing shallop makes her way
      Through the long day.
I cannot steer: I must not let her fill.

Halfway between the city and the island I
      Am bound for the city.
    The island had its terrifying
Pastures. There the bones of strangers lie
Unburied where we slew them without pity.
      We watched them, dead and dying,
      In the long light
And hugged the memory for many a night.

In flight from the unspeakable, we float
      Our household in a boat,
    Leaving behind us every grave
Of every ancestor we can recall.
The family mountains fade over our stern.
      The children, large and small,
      Whom we must save,
Turn their eyes forward to the land to learn.

Those children's hopes are here aboard with me,
            Adrift, adream, at sea,
        The peaks of home receding,
Alert for land across the wrinkled moat
Of ocean, without confidence or pity,
        While the strangely guided boat,
            Nobody heeding,
Moves its unknowing cargo toward the city.

Love, though I left you, smile on my return
            From the ancestral shrine
        Where blood will not again be spilled.
I would not travel now except to learn
More than the city teaches about sin:
        First, that that blood must be fulfilled;
            Second, that it is mine;
Third, that the island cannot take me in.

        Halfway between the city and the island I
        Am bound for the city.

THE IMMIGRANT'S APOLOGY

You think me citified, love?
Hard-shelled, headstrong,
Undoing all errors
With deftly trained fingers?

I am forced to step shrewdly
Through these byways perilous.
From every casement lewdly
Leans a crowd of faces of girls.

I am an islander, love,
Trained in taboos (Never touch
Hate with your left hand!),
Nourished on little and much,

Bred to believe
That ghosts guide bodies.
City ghosts do not bleed
With this our blood.

The journey here was long,
The boat, small,
Contrary winds, strong.
The sight of the towers was fearful.

Over the black pavement
Insect natives carry
Skeletons outside their flesh;
They click, they scurry.

My bones, love, lie in hiding.

LUCIFER ASHORE

One day as the girls and I were going to lunch
I spied my love that was, getting out of a taxi,
His gestures as heavy and familiar
As the sound of a hot night when no rain is coming.
He lugged his pride at arm's length in a briefcase
And stumped out of sight away along the street.
I watched, agog for the thunder that used to come
With his coming, and marvelled that his fall had drained
So much from each of us. What in the world
Was it that drove us to wriggle together in love
At dawn, on the island, before the city was heard of?
I must have wondered about it in his arms,
But now he struts the sidewalk like the others,
His footsteps clopping leather on cement;
And only I who knew him in the morning
Had warning of the fury in his eyes.

FOR AMPHIBIANS

I say my goodbyes
To orange peels, eggshells,
Chicken guts, celery,
Row a stroke homeward,
Then wait for gulls
To pick the stuff over.
Gulls are getting choosier
Here in the tideway,
But the sea never stops
Gulping and nibbling.

Bottles, bravest
Of all the garbage
I scuttle offshore,
End up mumbled
Down among the lobsters.
Tides or a loop of line
Sometimes unwater them:
What was clear, clouded.
Messages faded,
Contents doubtful.

Landsmen like me
Are shocked when sailors
Turn to the sea
As the place to retire
Whatever's unwanted
From soup to cadavers;
Yet they draw on its water
For all but libation
And bite without fear
Into fish that have eaten
Whatever we feed them.

The sun sinks down,
Crossed by a cormorant
Hastening homeward.
I turn to the oars

And row myself out of it,
Make my skiff fast,
Stamp feet on shore,
My pail rinsed clean
Of provisions, garbage,
Salt water, all.

To walk the path landward
I turn my back seaward.

ON THE ISLAND: THE DARKENED SUN

That day, the sun was twins.
He ate himself with shadow.
A black disc rubbed against
his red, like coins of different
currencies. Steeples split
like forks. Gulls flew backward
in bewilderment. The instant
the sun was wholly covered
by his sister, shadow
crawled across my face.
I stood in the depths
of my own darkness,
chilled with my own cold.

THEY THAT HAVE POWER TO HURT

Hand me the knife. There. See?
It has no harm in it.
The blade is merely steel,
Slightly chilly, as if
Shrinking away from itself.
The handle, comfortable
To any hand, can rest
In yours as well as mine.

Now feel the natural
Sag of your fingers, with
This guest aboard. Mankind
Was never itself until
It learned to take tools to task.
Knife is the tool of tools.
Who can play the man
Without regard for weapons?

Now the next step. Slicing,
Chopping, scooping
Are among the ways of women.
With this male friend to hand
Consider alternatives:
The sweep, the stab, the slash,
The parry, drawing lines
With a well-inked brush
In the pure color of blood;
And conclude: the tugging gesture
Of withdrawal and extrication.

These are only the first
Of lessons in harm's way.
Knives are a source of light
To explore the paths of the body.
Find a space for the edge
And your blade will never be blunted
But may probe and search the flesh
For the live parts, or even the dead,

To let the living out
For everyone to see.

The final lesson is this:
The man who holds the knife
Contains no more keenness
Than what he grasps.
Nor is the knife the ruler.
Your knife is neither tool
Nor weapon, neither a means
Nor an end. The knife is you.

LUNCH AT THE COQ D'OR

The place is called the Golden Cock. Napkins
Stand up like trumpets under every chin.
Each noon at table tycoons crow
And flap their wings around each other's shoulders.
Crumbling bread, I sip at the edge of whisky
Waiting for my man to embody himself
Until in time he shadows the head waiter
And plumps his bottom in the other chair.
Once he is seated with his alibis
We order drinks, we talk. His voice is rich.
Letters I had written him all winter
Had washed my mind of him, till Purdy,
Warm of heart and hearty of handshake,
Had shrunk into a signature, a stamp.
The fine print vanishes. I see him plain.
I know my man. Purdy's a hard-nosed man.
Another round for us. It's good to work
With such a man. 'Purdy,' I hear myself,
'It's good to work with you.' I raise
My arm, feathery in the dim light, and extend
Until the end of it brushes his padded shoulder.
'Purdy, how are you? How you doodle do?'

DANCE OF THE SHAKING SHEETS

Once we have discovered
How the heart grows old,
Leaving us no house
Against the cold,
We huddle for survival
And enlace
Body into body,
Face to face.

Hungry for compliance
That we once possessed
In the days of lap,
The days of breast,
We curl in the nest
Where we lately lay,
Savoring its softness
One more day.

There we know no hunger.
Surely more alive
Than when awake,
We shall survive
Stuttering rifles,
Deaf to the spit
Of angry bullets.
Let them hit.

Muffled under cover
We can bear
Any victim dying
Anywhere.
Rocking in the cradle
Of a lover's thighs
Softens the hunger
In her eyes.

Danger cannot penetrate
This womb.
Body, give us shelter.
Banish doom
Distant as the rifles
In the war
We refuse to study
Any more.

THE DESTROYER

Self-destruction works from the inside out.
We hear it scratching gently in the night
Like a mouse when the bedroom is too dark to see.
Somewhere we hear the crick of tooth on wood
And lie awake, imagining it inside
The book on the bedside table or behind
The lamp or peering from a drawer or shelf.
Turn light on it, it will disappear.
Lie in the dark, and it will scatter sleep.
Wait for the dawn; light shows there's nothing there
To finger or to tangle in a trap.
It comes and goes behind the walls we've built
As though we'd built the walls for nothing else
Except to hold, like Jericho, until
The trial. Then, with clang of ritual music,
The walls of self bow down their severed heads.

EASTER ISLAND: THE STATUES SPEAK

We are asleep, at peace. The grass has woven
A blanket for the fallen few who lie
Dreaming supine, watching the trade-wind clouds
Glide overhead. Our uplands are deserted.
Safe in settlements along the sea,
Shepherds avoid the hillsides we inhabit.

Now come newcomers, bringing means to force us
To rear up again, hillbound on rocky haunches,
Pitilessly to search the sea-surface
And guard the grassblades in their little seasons.
Aboard new rafts that snuffle past the reef
They make for landings on our lava beaches
To set about their plan for resurrection.
They hope by disinterring us to save
Themselves from meeting themselves at the fatal crossroads.

Our feet stood fathoms underground. Thin soil
Clothed us to our chins. How we hoped
To be forgotten! Now these new arrivals,
Who place unearthly burdens on God, unearth us.
They prop us upright for the hundredth time.
They will gladly let us sleep again
Once they have learned the reasons for our silence.

LIFE MASK

The self inscribes itself upon the face
With signs that age alone cannot complete
Before the mask has settled into place.

Appetite, sorrow, labor, all compete
For every pore of skin and ridge of meat.
The self inscribes itself upon the face.

Beauty fell back, already in retreat
Before the heart sat steady in its seat,
Before the mask could settle into place.

My face, a stranger in the mirror's neat
And family frame, had many friends to greet.
The self inscribes itself upon the face.

Deface, defy, distract, corrupt, or cheat,
Whatever the name, the face will show defeat
Before the mask has settled into place.

My paces not yet learned, I set my pace.
By forty, someone said, the tale's complete.
The self inscribes itself upon the face
Before the mask can settle into place.

RITES OF PASSAGE: 1946

Through a window the wind
Went leafing through my book
A chapter at a time.
A fearsome way to spend
Those Saturdays in June—
Stealing my hundredth look
Past the ice cream saloon
While studious prose and rhyme
Stood sentry to my crime.
The summer dusk inex-
Orably drew me where
The tyrants of my sex
Should stand and smoke and stare,
Shuffling outsize feet
At the corner of our street.
This summer was the first
That brought me to that town.
Our house was tense and small.
Those boys were large and brown.
No matter what the thirst
That drove me to the shop
Where they had gathered first,
I trembled lest their call
Might summon me to stop.
They whistled at the skirts
And laughed with hideous
Suggestion at a blush,
Still louder at a glance,
And felt their khaki pants.
They combed their oily mat
Of hair. They yawned and spat.
Their names I had not learned,
But others of like size
Had bullied me at school,
Connived with me in lies,
Had hurled and batted balls
With brilliance and surprise
And trained me in the rule

Of locker rooms and halls
Where victory was earned
And secret passion burned.
What was there to know?
The thunder that we heard,
That turned us limp and pale,
Our clumsy bones absurd,
Our fingers aching from
The need to touch and tell
The belly's muscled swell
That one was not enough
To sample smooth and rough,
To hold heat in the palm—
Ah, what was there to know?
Inveigling with a hand
At night, by day we spoke
In arrogance and brags,
In excrement and leer
And hunted down the weak
Like poisoned contraband.
The weak were always fags.
The strong were never queer.
Give me another smoke.
Look at these knockers here!
The girls we left behind
Lived in another age,
Walked gracefully as foam,
Looked down, were soft and still,
Giggled when put out
For lack of fist or shout.
They could not have been real.
No wrestling? No rage?
No laughter? Who can win
When there are only smiles?

Here in a strange town
I stand before a book
In a climate swollen with men
Who scuffle and leer outside

Across a street I cannot
Cross, a lifetime wide.
For nearly twenty years
I shall not turn again
To hang around with the boys,
To lean and take a look,
To whistle at my fears.
I shall burrow among women.

EURYDICE IN DARKNESS

Here far underground I can hear the trees
Still moving overhead where he, the poet,
Mourns. Let him stir stumps if he chooses.
Soon enough he'll sing his courage up
To penetrate the earth, clinging to that lyre
As though the world depended on it, and unstring
One after the other of my familiars,
(The three-headed lapdog, the boatman at the river,
The gaggle of furies, my Undertaker himself)
With instrument still twangling from the effort.
His fingers will be raw, but I'll be waiting
Dressed to kill and ready with a plan
He'll find acceptable. He'll turn his back
(Its every flabby muscle I have pinched
A thousand times) and clump along the tunnel,
Dead certain I shall follow him to sunlight.
And so I shall—murmuring at times,
Whining that he walks too fast, complaining
That he might at least give me a look
After such absence, brushing my breasts against him.
Not till the sunlight seeps in overhead
Will I tax him: a man and not a poet
Would have kept the country free of snakes
And left off that everlasting mooning and fiddling.
He could have prevented all this! And he might, please,
Give me a hand here, I'll fall with these sandals.
That's it! He turns from the light, his face engorged
With pity and self-pity. He thrusts out his hand,
And I shall dance away, my laughter dancing
Before me every mile of the way back home.

MAGPIE

Eight-toes, teetering
    Sabre unscabbarded,
        Bellying spinnaker

Fast to a fencepost,
    Gape your black bill
        In a squawk clean as kindling!

On, with a smother
    Of saw-toothed wingbeats,
        My piebald jolly-boat!

Surge hull down
    Past the crest of the ridge
        Where the wind breaks, breaks
        All day like foam.

EPITAPH FOR S.P.

Not as well cast
as most of her kind,
she guttered, burning
fast when she burned well,
smoking and flickering
at the bad patches.
(To burn evenly
was not her calling.
Oxygen came to her
in spasms.) She
gulped greedily,
filling her lungs
in every crevice.
Steady as long as
the air was steady,
she bent from the draft
beneath the door,
blazed up and up,
went out.

HAVING SAINTS

God has become too vast to pray to
for anything in particular. Not so saints.
Saints have at least a mouth to be remembered.
They did not build the world. They carried
only their own burdens. God is beyond us,
inhumanized by the long passage of time
since anybody saw Him. Even His mother
has stiffened over the centuries, until
the Church, recently, promoted her into heaven.
Saints have their presences on earth, thank God.
They carry keys or swords, they visit prisons
or in unhappy times have their breasts torn off
by pincers, even as you and I.
We're not ashamed to tell our small desires
to Paul or John or Nicholas or Teresa
in hope they needn't be passed on through channels.
We may even confess to them our grudges and panics.
A saint can be bargained with, done honor to
in exchange for favors granted, can be asked
to set his kindly parasol between
the searing sun and my poor eggshell head.
Prayers and pleading lie not so far apart
to give all praise to God, no plea for myself.
No god worth worshipping would listen to
a prayer that had no sources in desire;
but One who spins the galaxies is not
an Ear to whisper into. Lord, give us saints
even if we elect them for ourselves.

ONE OF THE MUSES

(For A.S.)

She sits beside a pool with pen and paper.
" 'A book should serve as an ax,' " she writes,
" 'for the frozen sea within us,' " and she turns
next to poems, chopped into the paper,
driftwood from a torrent, strokes clanging:

"I have taken pains to seek pain through the world.
Cataclysm is your only weather.
They say, the others, take cold but stay alive,
pain's a poor husband, they say delirium
crushes the breasts without caressing them,
death brings no blossoming nor impregnation.
What do they know? The world will turn to ice
if no one keeps the crystals from uniting,
and I am hot to break it up, with bleeding
knuckles if necessary. I must save the world
for the tides to wrestle in, and I shall ride."

She wallows in her howling sea of feeling,
enraptured, impaled on a thrusting mind—
her lonely lover, the last partner alive,
not yet drowned. Around, amid
the chambers of the brain, she dances him
to death, while he must grab and grin
but never shut his eyes for gazing at her.
That is her triumph. Pain gives her her joy,
for only pain will worship her completely
and never never take his girl for granted.

This dance follows no music: the dance
comes first, the music after. By the pool
she listens for the motions of the dance:
receding footsteps, memories of woe,
echoes of servitude. Slaves kneel in chains before her.
Away at the center of the pool is Self,
sinking in weightless silence to the depths,

hauling up to gasp above the surface
till it turns back again with bursting lungs
to thrust itself beneath the alien element
where she will be alone, enclosed, adored.

THE COLLECTOR

How the meadows dazzle this morning!
Every songbird's throat is gasping
To swallow deeper draughts of sunlight.
The fresh flowers gape as thirsty as the birds.

Like the web of a net my path crisscrosses
The piebald fields from wood to marsh
On the trail of plump lady slipper
Or openhearted blackeyed susan.

They flee me—lupine, arbutus, arethusa,
Dawn flowers fresh as the birds' dawn song—
Yet I am patient. There will be others.
Journeys end in lovers meeting.

Another day, another conquest:
The blush in the shadows, the crisp stem,
The velvet flesh against my fingers,
Head drooped prettily against my chest.

Hardly a field without its encounter!
Here are my prizes; here again, flowers
Taken in unlikely places and postures.
Some time I could tell you stories.

As the years pass, I take greater pleasure
In boasting where I found heart's-ease,
Forget-me-not, all the pretty creatures
That yearned so ardently from their dewy beds.

GIFTS

When I was a child, a heartstruck neighbor died
On her birthday. Dying was strange enough,
But what a way to choose to spend your birthday,
I thought, and what sort of a gift was this?
From time to time, people have done it since—
Dying in the environs of a celebration
As though they had picked out the day themselves.
Perhaps they had, one way or another,
Prayed for something to happen, and prayed wrong.
Sophocles, when old enough to die,
Suspected prayer and entered a caveat:
'Zeus, act kindly whether or not I pray;
And, though I plead for it, turn harm away.'
I keep a wary silence on my birthdays,
Make up no lists at Christmas, lie low
When asked what I *really* want. How should I know?
Best ask for gifts as though I had none coming.

PASSAGES FOR PURITANS

1.

A nose that sifts out all impurities
Keeps sensitive to scentlessness alone
And names all stronger pungencies impure.

2.

Life at the surface? It's invidious
That any skimming bird may pierce us through.
But to turn the back on ordinary air,
To follow the self inexorably downward,
Slough off the flesh in raptures of the deep
Where vision darkens like the bulging eyes
Of purblind fishes that have lived in caves?
Such cleanliness can crush the very bones.

3.

Those who purify their every motive
Will find themselves much cleaner for the effort.
They may take antiseptic satisfaction
In watching themselves in the frame of the mirror, washing.
They keep themselves clean at all costs, teetering
Thriftily on the near edge of orgasm,
Inquiring whether this thrust has any meaning.

4.

If life, as we admit in private life,
Is a dirty business, businessmen deny it
As they jostle in the stockyards with the others
And talk of life and death as "competition."
So do the commissars and delegates
Who talk of defense and aggressors, never of war;
Of freedom and peace, not wounded men or widows.
Words as cleansed as theirs exact a price
In dirty deeds, and, scentless, we perform them.

5.

We speak to signify. What bird can sing
Except with feet upon the swaying branch
That holds his nest, announcing to the world
That here he balances, here his children wait
To make their first, terrified forays
Across the dangerous air, where hawk or fox
May strike them bloodless? Therefore he sings.
Sings of the danger striking; of the sweet
Lift and totter of sustaining air;
Sings of the hunger in the blood and bone
And belly; sings of the pride in branch and nest;
Sings of the anger and the power to kill;
Sings of the mound of feathers on the hill.

PRETENDING TO BE ASLEEP

(1970)

> *Pythagoras would say to both: What is your warrant for valuing one part of my experience and rejecting the rest? . . . If I had done so, you would never have heard my name.*
>
> F. M. CORNFORD, *The Unwritten Philosophy*

FOR WILLIAM ABRAHAMS
AND IN MEMORY OF DUDLEY FITTS

AFTER BEING AWAY

When I shall die, in body
or mind, if you survive me,
give me my due. You know
I held no certain magic
and threw no light before me.
Searching out of pain
at first, then out of habit,
and out of self at last,
I stumbled on surprises
and managed to record them.
There's only one surprise—
to be alive—and that
may be forgotten daily
if daily not remembered.
Sometimes I remembered it.

You too, my love, have watched
each day for its surprises
and touched them as they happened.
Forgive me for inflicting
my pride on your surprises
and holding to the few
that were my sole possession.

Surprise we had together
in afternoon or evening
when we were close together
or even, often, parted.
I thank you for the thousand
surprises that you gave me,
not least the gift, unhinted
and endlessly surprising,
of never being absent.

MAKING MARKS

No two conventions of teeth behave alike.
Some chatter, grip, or slash. Others strike.
Thirty-two counters measure out our breath.
What other course for words but past the teeth?
The human body holds them at its height
Better to speak with, but the worse to bite.

Teeth hold the resonance for speech and song,
Which cannot rise past tunelessness for long
Unless teeth govern them to soar and lilt—
To pierce with love or hate up to the hilt.
Smiling, though soft in cheek, is hard in bone,
And sounds make words by trickling over stone
To give the tongue an edge to call its own.

Sounds are the stuff, yet letters are the knives
In each man's voice, the shape of what survives.
Dry bones alone can live, though fossilized
Forever. Let my words be recognized
As mine by the wear of their bite. They classify
The being that they once were brandished by
And the abrasives they were sharpened with.
This way he gnawed his life and grinned his death.

CASTAWAY

Out at sea, out of sight
of city or island, where waves
lap like tiles on a roof
reared over earth, there eyes
see nothing to see, there ears,
wave-wasted, have nothing to hear.
Only the sea of the blood
that sings forever behind
the ear and the eye, that recites
the syllables of spirit, now
makes itself heard or seen.
Old ocean parches the hide,
withers hands and fingers
and invites the drying flippers
to spread like fans, the fins
to gather into a tail,
and, smooth as a seal, the trunk
without so much as a whisper
to thrum its way to the bottom.
Only if heels, horniest
and hoofiest end of the body,
can keep their longing for land
may the mariner preserve
his true landworthiness;
kick them up, dig them in,
remembering earth to the last
where, alone, water has meaning.

Earth is always most
itself at the edge of the sea
where, rising at last from the salt,
Odysseus clambered the rocks
and, drinking deep of the spring,
his muscles wracked and torn,
shielded his salt hide
with a fresh green branch, and lay
beneath its shade to sleep.

THE PLEADERS

What are you going to do with us, who have
No edges, no talents, no discriminations,
Who hear no inner voices, who perceive
No visions of the future, no horizons?
We are among you; we are going to stay.

We crush, we drag, we heave, we draw the water
For you to spill. We gather together to listen
To your speeches, though your tongues run on so fast
We cannot follow, and your jokes dart in and out
Too quickly for our laughter to form itself.
We are your children, whom you treat like horses.

When crowds surge out into the streets
You have invited them; we run with them.
You give us order, speak on our behalf,
For we speak up too slowly to interrupt you.
We are the numbers ranked on your computers.
We are among you; we are going to stay.

If we knew how to pray to you, we'd pray
That you could listen long enough to listen
To what it is we think we want. We know
That what you think we want lies far away
From anything that has occurred to us.
We are your children, whom you treat like horses.

We are the eyes your eyes have never met.
We are the voice you will not wait to hear.
We are the part of you you have forgotten,
Or trampled out, or lost and wept to lose.
We are your children, whom you treat like horses.
We are among you; we are going to stay.

THE GUN HAND

You have been looking out for me. I held
A pistol to the ear of the Saigon captive.
It's been a busy year. I plugged the preacher
As he leaned on the lattice railing of his motel
And drilled the senator as he strode among the busboys.
I have aimed a thousand killers of all calibres
At television pictures, egg-hatted cops,
At the pulsing cartilage of a child's temple,
At the upstart cars that pass mine on the right.
I have squeezed so often you might think me weary,
But my hand is poised and clenched to squeeze again
At the next target of opportunity.

WHAT COUNTS

Our astronomic signallers are sure
That what they send is monitored Out There.
Whether the creatures who receive Earth's signals
Wear flesh or bone or neither, the reply
We get will be conveyed to us in numbers,
So those who man this world must be prepared
For grammar with no language. (A pulse, we call
Such signals? But that stands for blood with us.)

The words we use to amplify our numbers
Will count for little. Though they 'see the stars',
Our far communicants can send us nothing
That we have any names for—only numbers
Which in space-dialogue refer to nothing,
Not food or love, but only to themselves.
It could be heart alone that counts out there,
But without language we shall never know.

1968

For days the television seared our eyes
with images of the many-widowed family.
We crouched to stare at their loosened faces, their fingers
on rosaries, the hunched and harnessed shoulders.
(We starve for what survival has to teach us.)
Term after term their champions had been chosen,
served, shot down, reciting Aeschylus
and Tennyson. (" 'Tis not too late to seek
a newer world," and other familiar quotations.)

Too late, as usual, the latest killing
instructs us in our love for those who seek
more than we think of seeking. Soft in our seats
we watch the people of the long procession
reeling out across the summer landscape
to hide a body shredded and cold with bullets.
No one can hold his tongue: shrilled editorials,
New Year's resolutions, blurted promises
drown out the inner yelp of unmastered hounds
who press and snuffle hungrily along
the course this body leads us. At last, at night,
his remnants vanish in the grainy ground.

Before and after death we coursed that body.
No matter if words attacked, we could shrug them off,
but his image aroused our desire and nudged our hatred.
Slogging up mountains, seized by rapids, breasting
breakers, standing stripped naked by crowds,
his body sexed us. It revealed a self
our mirrors had never included. Gawky, controlled,
athletic in action, hectoring in speech,
it performed deeds that could have broken us
and left us with the trophies of last year's hunting—
whistles, grunts, imitated animals.

"Change," his body said—but when we heard
our voices speaking, they were not our voices.
His body has emptied the screens of our sight.
The people are not listening to voices.

THE ORIGIN OF SPECIES

The elements of flesh and flower
Take form in twig, in hand, in web.
Cast loose on nature's flow and ebb,
We mortals dabble for her power

And harry the shifting shapes of life
To know their truth but name our lie
With hints and handles for the eye
Like "unicorn" and "hippogriff."

Those elements of flesh and flower
Kindle new fire in cell and cell,
While, sealed within our citadel,
We name and number, curse and cower.

A WORD IN YOUR EAR
ON BEHALF OF INDIFFERENCE

History is sometimes salvaged by it, a civil servant
Who bows and smiles at weakness, at right and wrong;
At progress, poverty, peace and war; at victims,
Torture, and torturers. A skilled masseur,
Indifference smooths our faces into features
And lets our muscles work without rending each other.

Indifference-in-the-home lets tiring lovers
Share a warm bed between the defloration and
The signal for the soon-to-be-contested
Divorce to plunge both parties
In ice-water up to the arse.

Though we yell back and forth, "Let us erase our existence!"
"Let us scurry before the flailing winds of our senses!"
"Let us surrender into the hands of the forces!"
Indifference chimes in to discourage us from jumping.

My client gives us the power this side of death
To shackle ourselves, to live within our dimensions,
To ignore for hours at a time
The outrage and the dread
Of being no more than we are.

THE FORKED TONGUE

The double-dealer's house is built
With seam and scar, with stitch and patch.
His tongue invokes by sky and star
    The language of scratch.

Perjured in vocal clothes to match
His turban, surplice, or his kilt,
He tempers mind and mouth to purr
    The language of guilt.

Bicolored syntax in one quilt,
Two kinds of hate to chase and catch,
Two kinds of love: these agitate
    The language of scratch.

His brain, emboldened by the match
Of opposites, takes on a lilt
To croon whatever cadence fits
    The language of guilt.

Withdraw his hanger by its hilt
And wipe it bloodless; spring the latch;
And hear him sigh, alone, aloud,
    The language of scratch.

So crusted crime may heal and hatch
While golden syllables are spilt
To sing out false and crude and cold
    The language of guilt.

THE LOSING STRUGGLE

A Chinese word for landscape is made up of two characters meaning "mountains" and "waters."
ROSS TERRILL: *800,000,000*

To yield words easily gives pleasure
To the tongue that speeds their flow,
But, loosed, they linger on the surface
Like unexpected, unpenetrating rain.

Where are we to seek the words for life?
And how are we to see what must be seen
Before shaping our language to the sound of it?
What must be seen is every moment present

But hardly every moment seen. What I hear,
Like the muttering of a crowd, is seldom discerned
Although the murmur is never interrupted.
My body secretes against its rarest need.

When released, by lightning or alarum,
I can run like a deer, ravage like a lion, overhear
The creak of a mouse's toe on a wisp of straw.
Except for these times I sleep.

What are the repositories in myself
That bind me in the caverns of silence
And refuse to let me ramble at my will?
My ego stamps its foot at their refusal.

By the shore the sun embraces me.
The pleasures of water ripple through me
And take me by the singing throat.
The elms across the lake shine out like torches.

By another shore I watch the ocean scurry
Over its deeps of flounder and periwinkles,
Bearing its rockweed aloft like torches.
As its tide falls and the sandbar emerges, birds alight.

Here by the sea I cannot see as far as the mountains,
Nor do they loom over my shoulder as they once did.
Change is everything here, here everything changes,
Changes with the phases of the moon.

I have come to worship the sun, clouds, clarity,
And as deeply I distrust the moon.
I cannot bear the monthly flow of blood.
Tide and change corrupt the imagination.

I spin my fancies finer and finer,
A quota of gossamer every working day
From an old spider who does not care for flies
And webs it for the sake of the design.

My name is death. I freeze the world in light.
I see my arm, poised at my side to move,
But never moving; and my eye, my eye
Is fixed on what exists beyond existence.

AFTERWARDS

Sit down with me and rest,
    Beloved guest.
These gardens I have made
    Where summer shade
Is shaken from leaf to leaf.

Here is no desert where
    Death circles in the air.
Here the rich scent of fruit
    Has clambered from the root
To triumph on the bough.

Behind us lies the earth
    That tricked you into birth
And troubled you to death.
    Deny its names for grief
And anger now.

No longer flinch and stain
    To have it out with pain
Nor stretch your will to break
    What blood cannot forsake.
Now I have paid your debt.

I do not call you here
    To close your eyes with fear,
Despair, or counterfeit.
    Recline beneath the shade
Of gardens I have made.

PRETENDING TO BE ASLEEP

If a man could pass through Paradise in a dream,
and have a flower presented to him as a pledge that his
soul had really been there, and if he found that flower
in his hand when he awoke—Ay!—and what then?

COLERIDGE: *Anima Poetae*

1. *The Deserted Poet*

This part of the country is underpeopled.
Not a word waits in hiding under the ferns
To reach up for my hand and lead me out
Of myself. No words have passed this way this season:
I have forgotten even the sound of their footsteps
Whickering through the leaves at my approach.

Look at my face, never an honest one.
It covers my desertion by pretending
That words have never meant a thing to me.
This face settles for the lie. It puts on
Creases of feigned anger between the eyes,
Furrows of mock surprise across the brow.

I wear the mask of an actor who returns
From a long journey to find his wife and children dead.

2. *In the Dock*

Tried by the day, I stand condemned at night.
The evidence of years of fraud and shame
Waits until darkness to be brought to light.
Crime hangs from every letter of my name.

Each day conceals its treachery and blight
In places no defendant could disclaim:
Beneath the shirt, the mattress, out of sight
Behind the portrait smiling from its frame.

Night comes to sentence me. My second sight
Fixes me steadily within its aim
And squeezes slowly. With a shriek of fright
I fall forever from the cliffs of blame.

Watching my body vanish, I awake
To hear the sounds I never thought to make.

3.   *Under Protection*

One side wet and one side dry,
My skin walls out the world.
I am blockaded, only barely in touch.
Life stiffens and keeps its distance.

I coast in tides of light and cold
Past knife-edge noises and the smoke of cities.
The daily lives that shoulder the sound of my name
Seethe distantly across the flats of time.

I have dreamed myself into the streets
Of a village on market day. Aloft on the battlements
I command the town and prepare to seize
The contraband bartered by peddlers.

Boots dazzling, muscles like halyards,
My subordinates stand tiptoe in their barrack,
Braced at unblinking armed attention
For the clang of the summons to suppress disorder.

Out there the life could be just anyone's,
But it happens to be mine.
And do I govern it, pay taxes on it?
No, it is mine, but it offers me no friendship.
It surrounds me.

4. *The Flower of Sleep*

When danger strips the mind
And slithers toward my throat,
I slink away in hopes to stay
Alive, aloft, afloat.

I cringe from the land of light
To bury myself in sleep
As though a sea surrounded me
Of endless dark and deep.

There dreamers hand me flowers,
Presuming me to be dead.
'No reason why he'd choose to lie
Asleep in a death-bed.'

In this cradle of desperate rest
I snore away all fear—
The toppling tree, the storm at sea,
The Goddess striding near.

Such sleep does more than dream,
For when the sounds of day
Bring life to sight, I welcome light
To shudder my fear away.

But lately I dream of sleep,
Of wrecks and falling trees,
Of flowers laced around my waist
And grappling at my knees.

5. *The Public Garden*

I.

This public park and I are strangers.
Look at it; sit on its benches; no matter.
It sleeps though I am agog in its presence.

My turn to sleep. The park enters my privacy.
It wakes trembling in the spaces of my skull.
Its dry bones burst, its benches are my lovers.

III.

Each day the avenues I roam at night
Shut down when I awake, and no pretense
Of sleep will penetrate their spaces.
The visiting hours are over in the garden.

6. *The Visitant*

You make yourself known to me in surprising places:
A laundry or a bus, or late at my office desk
After the others have gone, or where I listen
To an unspoiled voice read out a familiar poem.

Distracted, clouded over, I am startled
Awake by your presence stealing up behind me
To draw my breath and raise your hands and clasp
The soft familiar palms over my eyes.

7. *Pretending to be Awake*

I am disgusted by the earthworks of my protection.
The clothes stink that curtain my nakedness,
And beneath the wool my flesh is beginning to fester.
I must tease my life awake that now lies sleeping.

Others stay awake in the dark by laceration,
By thrashing out at workers, lovers, children,
To keep their ears alert to the sound of sorrow.

Some plunge into the tolerance of women
Or paralyze the tendrils of their brains
Desiring visions beyond sleep or waking.

If I could tempt this sleeping life awake!
It shuns me now that sometime did me seek.

8. *The Cost of Pretending*

I would despise myself if I had the strength for it,
Would welcome the knife slitting the skin of my neck
As long as it did not falter and pour the blood.
Give me your hand, put it beneath my arm
Which closes on it, next to my heart. What
Do you hear of me? A steady beat, dull, leaden,
Irreversible. One who survives everything
Will shortly survive even himself.

9. *The Voices*

I know those voices. They are all mine.
Tuesday the infant,
Wednesday the child,
Thursday the grown man wheedling
In rut or yearning in prayer,
Friday the sexless ancient, dreaming of sex.

Through the country of sleep
The voice of my blood
Trickles like water over limestone ledges.
Tributaries borrow its *bel canto*
To stage-whisper their way through dreams
Or heroize the arias of nightmare.

The voice is me, whatever voice or stream,
The voice of history rising through my sources.

10. *First Voice: The Child*

Strange feet upon the stairs
Turn and walk this way.
I clothe myself in sleep
By shutting off my light.
They will not find the scent
Of hate on me tonight.

With one huge sigh, my chest
Moves easy, at the rate
Of every thief who breathes
More slowly than his guilt.
The door creaks open, but
My face, disguised in sleep,
Sings children's choruses.

The door has shut. The steps
Give way, descend the stairs.
The light, the book, emerge
From hiding. Like a bear
In blankets, all alert
For footsteps to ascend,
I lurk here in my lair.
They come? Then I'll pretend
Again to be asleep.

11. *Second Voice: The Youth*

What wakened me? Moon?
Rustle of willows?
A cry or creaking stair?
Or was it shadows
Troubling my sleep
With a tug at my pillows?

Out of the shadows
Where sleep had been hiding
An ominous parcel
Comes quietly sliding—
Charred bones and ashes
On the tide riding.

Who could the parent be
Of this delivery?
Hands cold as serpents
Fumble the frippery,
Wrench at the wrapping,
Pause and lie quivering.

No, let it lie there
Inside its adorning.
Now should I stand to arms
After such warning,
Or pace the aisles of night
Until morning?

12.   *Third Voice: The Widower*

The world has spread the word
That I am unworthy of it,
Crouching in lairs and caves
Pretending to be asleep.

First of the warnings: Love
Opened her eyes to me,
Then stopped her breath. No more
Pretending to be asleep.

Next came attentions, lavished
By divorcees and widows.
Though I took their bodies, mine
Pretended to be asleep.

Then came the nights, each darker
Than the one before. By night
I had no part to play.
By day I seemed asleep.

I know the sun by name.
This darkness may give ground
If I dream my way awake,
Pretending to be asleep.

13.   *Fourth Voice: The Grandmother*

I am an old woman living in a house beset with men.
It has been years since I heard a child
singing to itself.

These little men of mine are so little mine.
They live in the same dwelling but at a terrible distance.
They bring me their flowers but never notice me.
They wrestle with themselves,
with each other, father and son,
at all hours. I carry them platters of food.
They eat. They think themselves to be alone.
They walk like crustaceans.

There is no way for me to say, 'Awake.'
I must go on forever, smiling, serving, alert
for the accident of their waking.

Once young men stirred out of sleep
and smiled to find me naked beside them.
They gave me the flower of themselves,
the flower of their dream.
My little men do not yet know
they have been presented flowers.
They cannot recognize the face of the beloved
in their dream. How can they know,
unless they wake, that they have only
been pretending to be asleep?

14. *Possession*

Inside me lives someone who writes poems,
Someone who has no words but from time to time
Borrows my words, whirls them through the dance
Of his purposes, then returns them.

My only evidence for his existence
Comes when I find poems on my desk
Ready for me to revise.
                                    When did this happen?

Though I have never known who scribbled them
In secret, still I know my job.
I find them ready and waiting, I take over.
Possession they say is nine points in the poem.

OLD PHOTOGRAPH

Eight years dead, and dying
Many months before that, you leave me
No trace of yourself, except
These yellowing prints and some letters.
What do we know of the dead?
The needle of memory scratches
In the effort to remember.

Everything has been taken care of,
The papers are filed,
Most of the photographs mislaid
In a cigar-box.
Only this propped-up pose remains,
Rigid on the piano in pious memory.

While you were dying I shuddered
At every jolt of pain that shot through you,
Watched as you speechlessly
Contorted with a numb tongue
To speak of your dying.
I was told I would forget that
And retain the memory of you
In the sounds of your husky laughter,
Your charm in company,
The glee you took in never
Saying Goodbye on the telephone.

It isn't true. "True feeling
Leaves no memory," as Stendhal said.
It has left me nothing of you
But reminders that remind me of nothing.
Besides, only grief, sleeplessness,
Infant despair, betrayal.
These are you. I know nothing else
About you any more. I live behind glass,
Framed as tightly as your picture,
As frozen, as rigid, as blind.
How can I keep in touch
When there is nothing to touch?

23 September 1967

WORDS FOR MY FATHER

If God chooses you to have a son, tremble:
For just twelve years you may remain his father.
From twelve to twenty, try to be his teacher.
Thereafter you may hope to die his friend.

A MEXICAN VILLAGER

1. *Voice*
Your gorgeous voice soared
down the flumes
of the tumbling canyons.
Sentences and judgments rang out
with the clarity of air that knows little rain.
Giver, trainer of tongues,
even cottonwoods do not grow without water.
Your voice's notes were poetry, pity, war.
It restored bodies to the dead.
It taunted my mother, turning you into her child.
It sharpened the duellers' blades of long-forgotten rages.
It yearned for the doting and the pity of your children.

2. *Voyage*
I came to the sea after twenty years
and sailed to inquire
through all the trafficked harbors of the world
for news of my father's victories.
The voyage brought home little but pain,
messages garbled in transmission.
The air was dry and silent.
My father's eyes turned away
from the knowledge-swollen face of his son.

3. *Dead*
Later, when death began paying
its visits,
we were manacled by the knowledge
of how my mother, infuriatingly patient,
had bound us together.
On the voyages since, another ten years,
we have kept silence like Greeks

"carrying heavy urns full of the ashes of our ancestors."
More men and women have died.
We have not forgotten
your mother's rectitude, her shabby flirtatious plumage,
nor your father, whose testament
was leaner than you desired—as every father's is.
His blood has scalded you
but you need not share his blame.
Give him your blessing.

4. *Road*
I walk forward in the afternoon of dying
along the road of words, cruel to the feet.
The dry tawny hills below your orchard
stretch away without shade or the sound of water.
Not yet in sight of you, I hear your
cough, your parched and grating throat.
Shall I answer the question you are sure to ask?
If you are Odysseus, my son, come back,
Give me some proof, a sign to make me sure.
I have three signs: the scar, the trees, the words.
The scar of our parting, which has never healed.
The trees you planted, felled, buried under rubble.
The love we shared, carried by words only.
Deeds overwhelmed us.

5. *Words*
Words need not always fail.
No matter how seldom
we gather ourselves
to gather our hopes
into flocks, herding them before us
to huddle in their pens,
they are our dearest gift from this sparse soil,
the locked and grudging earth. They are
our servants, our sacrifice, our pledges.

Your gift to me
is my gift to you.

THE LAST WORD

When I saw your head bow, I knew I had beaten you.
You shed no tears—not near me—but held your neck
Bare for the blow I had been too frightened
Ever to deliver, even in words. And now,
In spite of me, plummeting it came.
Frozen we both waited for its fall.

Most of what you gave me I have forgotten
With my mind but taken into my body,
But this I remember well: the bones of your neck
And the strain in my shoulders as I heaved up that huge
Double blade and snapped my wrists to swing
The handle down and heard the axe's edge
Nick through your flesh and creak into the block.

THE TWO OF YOU

I

Your face is tense as wire within a wire
    When you consent to bed with sunlight flying.
The dervish flashes up into the fire.
    Not to be lost to love is to be dying.

Molten and greedy, quivering in my arms,
    You gnaw, you tear, you moan beneath my prying.
Our veins are full of sunlight as a field.
    Not to be lost to love is to be dying.

These fearful bodies rage against our will—
    Our love is truth and leaves no room for lying.
These stones, these walls, this house, this windowsill
    Are not to be lost. To love is to be dying.

II

Outdoors the breeze blows childlike, notwithstanding
    Tomorrow it could be carrying sounds of war.
As we pass, we turn toward each other,
    Lovers in a bed.

We preserve house-plants, growing creatures,
    By constancy of warmth. In their season
Light airs are given entrance. We exclude only
    The brazen airs that turn flesh into stone.

Nourished by our senses and attentions
    This house will open up into a palace
Where children dress themselves in royal robes
    And swagger with the certainty of angels.

To hear one another's voices without speaking
    Makes up the music of this house. The time
Of storms is welcomed as a penance.
    This house is silent and fragile as God.

CALYPSO

She found him facing out into the fog
At the edge of the sea, stooping, winnowing
Stones with all the care of the demented,
Hurling them into the murk, low along
The surface, skipping them like petrels.
He wandered by the shore, halting and stooping,
Leaning abruptly for additional
Hates to send spinning out to sea.
She watched from the cliff over his restlessness
And ached to hold him in her arms—held
Herself away from him, for an embrace
Would only remind his body of its bruises.
Hobbling a step, stooping, sorting the stones,
Hurling them again, as though he hoped
To force them, slippery beneath the sea,
To draw him after them, he threw and threw.
The shore wind whipped the bracken by the path,
Pressed out against the fog which yielded to it
And took it in and closed and gave no ground.
A woman could do nothing for him now,
Though she had known for months that this was coming—
Long before he guessed, even before
She herself could have put it into words—
His occupation gone, his enterprise swallowed.
The tide was out, the stones lay high and dry.
Terns chirruped in the fog along the shore.
The fog pressed on the land a little closer
And she could scarcely see him now, while he
Would never look back to where she stood behind him,
Just as he would never know that she
Had watched him strive, delude himself, and fail,
Had known all his evasions and deceits,
His minor infidelities, his hopes
That this time shabbiness would go unnoticed.
The only way to show her love for him
Was learning how to stand unseen
Until he chose to notice her—to laugh
Or storm or touch her breast or ask for food

And, though she was invisible, to smile for her.
Now in the fog he'd wandered farther off
Than she had ever lost him, yet she still
Was more aware of him and his despair
Than fog and sea and wind and stones together.
And so she turned, knowing herself helpless,
Leaving her man to men's devices, and the wind
Struck at her face as she walked weeping home.

STUMPS

The field is studded with their thousand lives.
All that is left of all that tracery
Pokes through the goldenrod in amputations
Too short to see, too tall to be mown over.
Their knuckles sprout new fingers every April.
I go my rounds in August trimming them back.
The roots, now elderly, are just as far
Involved in growing as they ever were,
But their suckers are sickly and cannot survive
Unless they're given help by God or me.

After a year or two of this flirtation
I snap trees off by hand which saw and axe
Once needed all their edges to bring down.
Reason could lull these lives to a merciful end,
But I as owner claim the dark indulgence
Of giving them a chance to sprout once more.
Crops like mine are not so much planted as buried.

WALKING THE BOUNDARIES

(*1974*)

FOR ANGUS AND LESLEY

IS ANYTHING WRONG?

(For Margaret Atwood)

I do not know what I mean. Perhaps you know.
These lilypads, these ghostly gingkos and herons
stretch up their presences from the anti-world.
I live and move among visions; I hold
my being in my hands and cannot recognize it:
what sort of creature am I inside of?
Pressing closer to the knowledge
that there is no knowledge, that our world
is visions, shadows, I hear it rumored
that perhaps, who knows, we are living in a cave?

DOORS

I know what lies behind them in the attic.
I have been filling its dusty corners for years.
Those pigskin suitcases, with ancient labels
from Karlsbad or København, no longer fit
even for storing woollens, have been covering
for the wrong man.
Toys with a leg broken,
cartons of dead letters, not one of these
means a thing now except as part of me.

I am bursting, dying.
My body is broken.
The rooms might be as empty without me
as they are already empty of the dead;
and I am even emptier than the rooms,
for I contain them.
I am not a plant, I am dying.
There is no bud-time for me, no seed-time.
I am a chieftain without a tribe,
a lover without a bed.
My arms fly at my side, my knuckles pop.

A woman is listening to me.
She leans forward, sets her hand on my knee.
Her eyes shine.
She listens, she understands.
I cannot do it without her.
Pascal said the greatest fear in life
is the fear of sitting quietly in a room alone.

I peer up the stairs. I strike a note.
There is no one there to see, to hear,
under the rafters. The loneliness
in this last room is infinite.
I have shut my past in here
behind the doors I have closed,
and all the rooms contain me.

THE HEROINE

She was one of the few I can speak of who believed
in personal destiny; the only one who swore
by holy writ that death was worth gambling on;
the meanest spirit to claim a martyrdom
since sainthood ended. What a cunning braggart
she was, a frailty who pictured herself
as a rider of skis, of waves, of men, of horses.
She lugged about a pessary in her purse
like a baloney sandwich in a lunchbox
and referred to Dylan Thomas and Dostoevski
in the tone of voice reserved for former lovers.
Breck hair, white scarves, clean flesh, hard muscles,
sun-worship, and a trough of molten and remorseless work.

I've seen her love-letters—those she wrote
to other men while she was using me—
and her hate-letters—those she wrote
to me while she was using them—but only once
or twice her tiny writing in a different hand,
tilted across the page, wounded, but credible
as the early morning trail of half an earthworm,
speaking of her selfhood in the tiny voice
that had been hers as a child, hers once as a girl, hers, hers.
In the usual rooms she spoke in a voice more humble
than the one she wrote in, cozening her larynx
to belie the costumes of ambition, clothes
Mother had dressed her in to go to school.
In saddle shoes and pageboy bob, disguised
as Betty Boop, inculcable, unresisting,
she set out bait for poets and professors.
She was as innocuous as Lenin in Switzerland.

The acrid sun tugs at her shrinking skin.
Out in the desert, blankeyed from deceptions,
she hugs herself to herself, learns how to ride,
to hate, to write, to broadcast, to give milk.
Her husband and her children, grating on her,
teach her a little more of how humans do it,

of how humanity must learn to sleep.
But then the tiny voice within her voice
struck up its canticle of loathing for
ambition's wigs and masks. Off with disguises!
Snarling and sobbing like an orchestra,
she levelled the forests of ego,
whirling around her bare blonde head
a sword as holy as a samurai's.

ASKING NOTHING

The words carry themselves as carefully
as a muscular woman tricked out in sequins
walking a high wire.
I ask nothing of them, I only
set them in motion as gently as feathers.
Birds exert themselves more than the words do.
Hunger compels them, they cannot choose but fly.
Words, who seek no food for themselves,
follow a leader they have not chosen
in an order they have hit upon without deciding.
Only those words are admitted that speak of their speaker.
Whether they speak well or ill of me
is not their business nor even mine.
Their only need is, they should speak a language.
Having walked a way, they return to silence,
leaving only the memory of the drum-roll,
the sequins, the spotlight, the high wire.

EMBRACES

1. *The First Stranger*

She wants his way! He's won! His will, set free,
canters inside his head, and fingers grip;
she nestles close, suggests with tooth and lip
the time is past for play;
her hands, the bolder pair, direct his way;
he is astonished at such avidness,
shrugs out onto the plain of nakedness
to find her there, an offering; he nears
what cannot be reversed; he summons in
his wits to guide his memory and smears
bookish caresses on her stranger skin
until her breath reminds him: it is She.

2. *Stranger Still*

Puffed like a silken sleeve, your body
dimples under my sausage fingers
as we give over to double dreaming,
slithering over each other in silence,
except for the sound of separate gasping,
to give it to each other here, this body
I call mine grappling with the one you call yours,
wrapped in summer sheets, wet
with sweat and (soon to be) with semen,
giving it, giving it, giving it
to the humped and whimpering stranger
who soon will lie beside me, knowing only
I too am wet, I too am awake.

3. *Family Reunion*

Dreaming of scattering mists, I awake
to the warmth of a breathing and browsing.
My hand is touched. A shoulder tingles.
A breast is tapestried over with hair.
No dream, no dream.
Our bed puts by the fragrance of sleep
to take on the liquor and odor of waking.
The hand rambles. I swim out of myself
into the welcoming lake of your flesh.
Fractiousness and the humdrum spatter
of chattels and children
of meals and mercy
go shying away.
Our bones go begging, breathing like bells.
We rise through the plaster ceiling,
majestic as two full moons,
till, far off, tenderly as a heron circling,
unaware that a footfall has been chosen,
we drift back through the bivouacs of darkness,
breathing easy.
We alight on the earth,
enter the house,
sigh deep down into the dens of our bodies.

THE OBITUARY WRITER

There are two voices, and the first voice says, "Write!"
And the second voice says, "For whom? . . .
And the first voice says, "For the dead whom thou didst love."
JOHN BERRYMAN, 1968, QUOTING KIERKEGAARD,
WHO IN TURN IS QUOTING HAMANN.

When I reach out towards the body of happiness,
a hoarse voice warns me off: "No no. Not *you*."
It must be the obituary writer,
the one who scrambled into print the hour
each poet died, always the first to know.
When off obits. he spoke for Henry, defendant.
He waved goodbye and jumped from a high bridge
and clattered dead on the ice of the Mississippi.
I felt the fall coming all the way to Rome
where I took up pen and paper, an obituary
writer's obituary writer. Quickly death spoke,
shouting in its own hoarse voice. Outside,
across Largo Febo, barely out of eyeshot,
an old mad woman had unmouthed her teeth
to save them for another life. In bib and blanket,
with stockings swathing her ankles, she set her body
adrift from the fourth-floor windowsill. She encountered
the January pavement with a cry.
Soon the *polizia* were snapping photos.
Neighbors huddled together in knots, muttering,
their faces gray as hers. We all mooned over
the swollen object laid out on the cobbles.
The skull was crushed. The flung hands had turned purple.
No one knew her name, least of all the papers.

Dead Henry, better known to all the papers,
was noted alive because, sober, he suffered the shakes.
Drunk, he shrieked and ranted. Who could stand
to stay in the room with him? Not prissy me,
who couldn't abide the hoo-ha, the abasement,
nor my own flinching from his open pain.
His head was full of everybody's death.
His pants sagged, his fly gaped, his hullaballoos

of falling-down drunkenness were an insult to the brain
no matter how hotly and crisply he employed
hangover time for his mettlesome minstrel show
of dreams, obituaries, exhalations.

Some obituary this is: not that of a friend
nor even of an accountant for the fact
of death, of bodies falling alive from heights
in January and landing dead. Admit
that poetry is one of the dangerous trades.
No matter how many we know who have been goaded
by its black promises to deliver
their bodies to the blue snowdrift of death,
it was not poetry, but life, they died of.
Since the day that the old woman took her teeth out
and John the master minstrel turned away
from the gravel of his brother Henry's voice,
there has been no avoiding this obituary.

INTO THE FUTURE

Standing here just short of the corner,
I grope with fingertips
against the rasping surface of brick.
If it had handholds I would hang on.
One move could ruin everything.
They would find my blood running down the wall.

In times like these
one never retraces steps. Forward
is the only direction. Beyond this corner
the wind gusts cold, coughing wave-
whirls of dust along Michigan Avenue.
If I let go and turn the corner
what will come at me from my blind side?
A newspaper clutches my leg and forces me on.

POEM OF FORCE

Sacrifices meant nothing to *me*.
I loved every inch of him: his wrestler's muscles,
his tanks and his missiles naked as mine.
How I kissed his statesman fingers
and his soldier toes!
I tattooed on his breast
the imprint of my body.
Even while sleeping or drunk I guarded
chest, notch, and boundary against his skirmishes.
Never have I understood an ally so well.
He is my darling wolverine.
Keeping him fed full with nourishing rations,
I surmount him like a tower, and he smiles
in gratitude as I draw black blood
from the bodies of his children.

AT THE CLOSE

We limp along the shoreline
scuffling and probing for fish
alert enough to eat. Each time
stupefaction chokes us, we stare for breath
out across the sea, abloom
with a jungle of algae.

Birds and hot-breathing beasts are few.
Reptiles have the best of it,
preying on the tumbled bodies
of gulls, on fish that breach
the tangled surface of the sea.
After dark, thallophytes
whisper the truth.

Nights are warmer than formerly.
Everything takes forever—
writing, walking, even stooping,
most of all sleeping.

(I cannot snooze for an hour
without dreaming of drowning.)
At greasy daybreak our faces flush,
and we grow giddy and quarrelsome.

Still, we have more to marvel at
than ever, especially sunsets.
The earth hangs on to air
enough only to breathe—none
to make love, none to make war.
The planet hisses with oxygen.

WALKING THE BOUNDARIES

1. *West, by the Road*

Now swift swallows have flown for the winter.
The last pears have fallen.
Maples, huddled close in the swamp,
slip off their leaves
and lay bare the shaggy cliffwall.
Twigs in damp tangles under
the sagging grasses
abandon themselves to rot,
food for beetles.
Hardiest of their generation, wry apples
clutch at gnarled branches
as long as the wind will let them.

The sumac's crimson seedpods cringe
while the air unleashes the first
fast rangers of milkweed.
Under the deep beeches
in leafmold crevices
autumn phalluses
rise up in a single night from
forgotten woodpiles.
The screech of a bluejay batters
naked oak trunks, scattering
bleached goldfinches
wherever they gather on thistles.
The junco's tail flashes
in the cedar. He sings
of two pebbles chipping against one another.

Toppling grasses and unsteady leaves
tolerate the chickadee's scramble
through the drowsy apertures of autumn
toward the house
whose chimney sighs grey woodsmoke
and panes of glass smile earlier each evening.
Roots hunch and contract, their blood runs thin.

They hold forearms
stiff against the wind, while
castaway stones
plunge fistlike for winter
into the ground's gravelled belly.

Sighing, chuckling, the minnow-busy
creek's summer-warm tides,
heartbeat of the sea,
steam and scurry.
The thatch of the marsh holds hard:
it crouches down on matted fibers
to quake at air but yield its seed to water.
Come January, grumbling glaciers
will walk uphill in the arms
of northeast gales to shear
a year's marsh hay
and macerate against the granite
piers of the bridge
the buried shells of snails.

Moles burrow down to the frostline.
Starlings hang on in holes
hard-won from woodpeckers.
Squirrels, walled up between
skyscrapers of hickory nuts (all
stolen except for a handful
of windfalls wrapped in their husks)
duck down under the barn.

Snow is coming. Snow
is coming. All but birds
will be buried. Water will
absent itself till spring,
while earth locks up into its mineral meaning.
Only yesterday we breathed a world
of liquor and seed. It hardens now.
The little animals lie panting,
sleepless, winterless,
anticipating drift and flake,
awaiting the crackle of frozen meat

upon the tongue. Their lungs
bloom like flowers
at the alienation of the air.

2. *South, by the Wall*

The trees are choiring their light at the house.
A new-minted copper beech stands burnished
at its greening sister's side
crying aloud with the zeal of its leaves,
which have unfolded this morning like lemur's
fingers. In the swamp, ferns uncurl
their bedsprings. The meadow grass,
as thick as fur, crowds on itself
to gobble up yesterday's rain.

No passageway is left in the pasture
for large-footed beasts, only room for speckled
clutches of eggs and the tender claws
of new-hatched fawn-spotted pheasant,
hiding and scuttling between the scented
trunks of grass-stalk and grass-stalk.
Spiderwebs balloon with bubbles of dew
while their mistresses stopple their breathing-tubes,
travelling upward and down,
inching and testing.

As soon as the sun has ripened
toward the hammered gold of sunset,
it departs for its nightly reception
in the West, leaving the sky all pearls.
Mice and moles, peepers and woodcock,
speak up in twittering singsongs.
Robins yodel. Owls and night-herons
scream and crawk.

Out of sight of the sun the plants
lie quiet. They snuff their inner candles

as the moon combs through fledgling trees
to ruffle the landscape and frost their leaves
with the filigree of moonshine.
This is the time for sleep.
We will feed even better tomorrow, and, after
the sun mounts high, breed till our brains burst
with the bluebell music of flickers and grackles.

3. *East, by the Cliff*

The pasture, freckled with patches
of elderly snow, flutters pale flags
of martyred goldenrod. Ice pokes and clutches
into the female cleft of the Indian rock.
From high vantage in our eldest hickory
jays engage in an antiphony
of creditable outrage
against their rivals the crows
who station themselves in the maples.

My breath is glue in my nostrils.
Mere air holds the sleeping marsh
solidly in chains, it crumples
the recent thaw's ruts
into hogback ridges
that the sun when it waxes
will take much trouble
to melt down again
into March mud.

Barren as an unlocated satellite,
this moment is dustless and rigid.
Only the gurgle and scurry
of blood-salt tides can
irrigate these badlands,
scatter the ice-floes, patiently flush
the mud-bottomed creeks, never mind remorse,
into the patiently receptive sea.

The barking of bored dogs
rattles the hard hillside.
The jays protest, chickadees chatter,
fierce finches whimper.
Pent and braggart geese
in my neighbor's corral
cackle echoes against
my iced-over windowpanes.

Our beechwoods have given up
their ghosts to mushrooms.
Plumes from grosgrain chimneys
remind me with woodsmoke
how, crisply thrusting and stretching,
roots and bowed branches conveyed
quick currents of sap
through the longtime noontimes
of longago summers.

A pewter-colored sky
tightens up into zinc
as the momentary day flickers
toward sundown. Breath from the South
drops heathery hints of a promise,
but the North rides back in its tracks
at the near edge of dark to retract it.

This is the season of waiting for light,
of electric nights, of unrecognized footprints.
Wan woodpiles and slumbering straw
nurse reliquaries of calories
against the scorch of wind and the hiss of snow.
They sing lullabies across the chasm
between this dangerous land
and the whispering sun.

4. *The Woodcock*

Inside my human walls I sit surrounded
by scurrying music. Voices sing *Kyrie*.
My eyesight ranges out across the field.
Those acres tolerate us as their maker does,
suffering denials without a sound,
courtesies and rain without a smile.
They've settled for the edge of land and sea.
Downstream, northerly, the restless waters
search up the creek twice every day
and twice a day back off to leave it dry.
At certain tides the place has the look of an island;
at others, a desert of cold mud. Crops germinate
to feed the appetites of muskrat and mackerel.
This is saltmarsh country, two-way country,
no-man's land for gill beasts and lung beasts.
Its frontiers meander, liquefied, unmeasured.

Color fades out of the field as though the sun
had dipped into the earth to stain the clouds.
Indoors the singers climb the scale from mercy
to glory, from belief past blessing to
a resolution—the unimaginable plea
that a Lamb should Grant us Peace—and then are silent.
Over the land and sea, air cools and hardens.
A thrush sings its Goodnight. Among the maples
of the swamp, peepers fiddle their shrill chorus,
toads who have somewhere learned to sing like birds.
Here, where coastline edges off the forest
and the woodland's freshet leavings leak away
to modify the high tide's appetite,
I hear the woodcock's sundown declaration
that he too is ready to sing. There's light enough
left for me to see the dumpy body
as it shuffles among the tufts of last year's grass,
restless and ready for nightflight. Hear the blare
of his tiny trumpet, so sharp a sound that he
must hunch his shoulders to squeeze it out. Again

and again his music sends the lively word
to the edge of the woods and out across the marsh
as though this Orpheus could command his voice
to travel back and forth between the worlds
just as his wondrous delicate bill can probe
the soggy earth for worms.
                      Now we have arrived
at the edge of darkness, and the woodcock, darkened,
leaps aloft with a whirr of wings. Wings?
No, music—his voice, he is singing! He rises up
past the dark treetops to the graying sky.
As he leaves the earth his song ascends
higher and higher, pitch upon pitch, spiral
after spiral. At last, at the top of his helix
three hundred feet or more, it is enough,
he can rise no farther on the updraft of this song,
he has reached a boundary. He starts to fall,
he topples from the peak, repulsed by sky,
he dips zigzag and loops and twitters earthward,
his song hot on the wingbeats of his flight,
coiling in chirrups of retreating tailspin.
Plunge and flutter. Silence. He glides
from the edge of light across the edge of dark
to alight upon the very shadowed patch
of earth from which the night had lifted him.
A pause for breath. He trumpets out a warning
that *this* was not a failure. He collects
himself to ascend again, to reach beyond
the edge of the habitable world, beyond
his limits of heaviness and incarnation.

Gills dried up long since, useless on land.
Fins flowered into three-toed featherweight
tuckaway talons for pouncing and perching.
The brain, too massive to fly very far with,
dwindled in birds once flippers became wings
and danger need no longer be outwitted
but merely flown away from, left behind.
How much is left behind at boundaries!
Arising from the sea we lost our lightness.
Thought took us to the woods, where vision blurred,

for sight and mind do not take wing together.
Body at least is bound within a landscape,
an earth that holds us fastened to the seasons
for food and footing, birth and burial.
Regardless of the gifts we've left behind
and all the boundaries we cannot cross,
some power lets us press beyond our powers:
echoes of wind, of ebb and flow, of heartbeat,
singing that trickles landward with the waters,
music that clambers skyward through the dark.

CALL SIGN AQUARIUS

The water I am made of,
free-standing, unencumbered,
has learned to pronounce me and
call me watercourse. Call me:

a hunched and encroaching darkness
ozone clogging the nostrils
a blinding pounce of light
a chuckle of distant thunder
a clod sucking the spatter
and satisfaction of the storm
a pasture glazed with dandelions
and lupines
a bare shouldered sun
in a brisk and clarified sky
songs of a thrush spiralling up
to carol darkness into the drenched woods

In the silence of this white-plastered room,
alone and dry, deranged,
I hum like a transistor with the codes
of faraway weather.

MOTLEY

Hairband, homespun, opera-hat, afghan,
turtleneck, sheepskin, catskin, buckskin,
denim, dimity, beadwork, braidwork,
rags ripped off from old six-reelers—

all serve as signals to allies and enemies
that Whatintheworld may be taking the air.
Could he be banker, butcher, broker,
madman, marauder, masquerader?

Men who wear ascots, waistcoats, cheviots
are ostracized as doctors, lawyers, palaverers,
rich men and thieves—uncurious costumes!

Young men, beggar men, brawny men saunter
in pigskin, lambskin, desert boots, sandalslippers,
hairshirts and hiphuggers. Others lay footbones
bare to the broken glass, dogshit, chewing gum,
sleep in the park with guitar cases, rucksacks,
stretched on the sidewalk, curbside, fenderwise.

Whether they're indoors, outcast, uptight,
grant them their groin bulges, hairlines, hiplines,
toenails, kneecaps, beardstubble, sticknipples,
grant them their armpits, cockpits, spitballs,
precious possessions, all body-portable.

Better go dogsbody, jackanapes, bareass
than strut through Necropolis unrecognizable,
sexless, seducible, deeply disguisable!

THE DANCE OF THE HOURS
or, *It's a Living*

Each hour of workaday fits just as well
as my old tweed jacket which has taken years
to learn to sag its shoulders. Sixty thousand
hours have rubbed up this telephone, tattooed
the roller of the typewriter. O shelves
and drawers, what purple uprisings you've stacked
into submission! For you I've herded papers
in and out to be disposed of elsewhere—
say in the crypt, say in the dead file.
I cling to my perch between the two baskets,
what a responsible spot. I'm here to keep
things that come *In* from getting *Out* too soon.
No one will liberate those memoranda
ranked up behind their fellows in the file
unless it be the moth that flickers, remembering
the odor of our bargain. We've forged a set
of deeds, wills, seasons, my hours and I.
We grow together in one tree, sparing and spending.
We never speak of what has passed between us.
We stare at one another through a window
and wonder which will be the first to sell.

BED TIME

Few beds are stonier than one shared by a sleeper
and a waker who stares into the dark
listening to the house breathe. Children
sigh, dogs snore, clocks tick, radiators mutter.
Love past, he lies vacant. Bed carries him
to countries that his body will never visit,
regions where his mind cannot drink the water.

Feet up. Blood trickles through his head
to pass between Horn Gate and Ivory Gate.
Sleep pilot, dreamer, flying Dutchman,
he steers his ticktock course between chills and fever,
bound out of Birthport for Lovepool and Death Haven.

Love past! Clandestine beds in borrowed apartments.
Fern beds, pine needles, beds for *porcheria*,
beds whose springs crumpled from exuberance
or rattled with anger, beds whose backs bent
from nightly throes of union and reunion.
"O bed, where first I loosed my virgin girdle . . ."
She fell upon her knees and kissed the bed.

As in a hospital where he awaits in bed
the next day's condescension of doctors,
he bleeds broken promises. Is it sailing time
for the ship of fools, the ship of the dead?
Pain lightning flickers and spatters
the four-cornered flatland of his life,
but what else is there to fall back on?
In bed we depend upon nothing but bed.

DARK HOUSES

For Edward Davison (1970–1898)

I shall come back at last,
In this dark house to die.
EDWARD DAVISON, 1919

1. *At Seventy-One. New York.*

Words have finally failed this balloon of a body,
White as a side of bacon, cold as the plank
It heightens like foothills under a sheet in the morgue.
Inside it, living, smoldered poetry
Like January wasps that stir in summer houses.
Parched past a trickle now, his will had wrestled
Headlong through the pastures of his youth
In floods of love. He squandered it, spent it on girls
Who took his rings and sold them for a ribbon,
Leaving him petulance and loyalty
As stones in drought, no longer bathed by love.
In spite of years and years of wearing down,
The words whose slave he was could still surprise him.
Lying half-blind, his lips alive with poems,
In his delirium his voice cried out again
With "Elsie Marley", "The Tyger", "O Mistress Mine",
'Led by a blind and teachit by a bairn'.
From the first breath in Glasgow to the last
Shudder in Mount Sinai Hospital,
Words, and the songs of words, convinced his life.
No words go walking in a darkened house.

2. *At Fifty. Pennsylvania.*

His days of life grew drier with the years
Or dwindled into place-names on a map.
In his own eyes, what cracks across the glass,
Betrayals he had given and received?

Lord, I am not worthy to sit at Thy table.
He downed each whisky like a punishment
To keep his heart from thumping with the shame
Of memory and waste. 'The parable of the talents
Lies on my conscience like a heavy weight.'
Buried was the hate of his treacherous father
In old men whom he loved. He worked to win,
And won, their praise, as heavy as a father's,
But praise from such could never quite be trusted.
Buried, buried were all his loves and flowers
In the woman who never calmed him but inflamed
His anger. O buried deep inside inside
But bursting out in coughs that stretched and tore
His chest and neck in the tempest of his rage,
Dry places racked him with a daily taste
Of all that wrestles poetry to earth.

3.   *At Forty. Colorado.*

Hard by these mountains, cottonwoods and creeks,
He pitched his camp, the woman at his side,
And basked in the dry light of his latest father—
President, chief scholar, neighbor, friend.
The world of London letters grew more faint,
But students clustered round. His voice, reciting,
Drew them to poetry as to a mass.
What he saw kindled in their faces helped
Him hope for recompense from poetry,
For poetry is what he spent for them.
She would not wind her arms around his arms
Nor would he cleave to her, forsaking others.
Exiled, admired, content and yet dismayed,
He came into his own as son and father
Just as he, knowingly, went down as poet.
Without the nourishment of loneliness
Or lovers to betray him, poetry
Turned from his bed, his page, but not his life.
Desertion is not charged in this affair.

4. *At Thirty. On Tour.*

His heart's love now laid bare, he gives pursuit
Across an ocean, putting her to proof.
She flies before him, hesitates, surrenders,
But only for the moment. He must set
His mark on her, let her not disappear,
For she will never answer all his letters.
Sinking his past behind him, he embarks
On the *Britannic Sea* and lands, surprised,
At Montreal to garner his reward.
In wilderness, beside the Rangeley Lakes,
Amid the barbershops and alien corn,
He finds her. Is it he she's waiting for?
Her eyes more than her voice confess she's true.
Scanning a whole new continent for the prize
He values most, the treasure that eludes him,
He searches eagerly as ever for
The faithful woman, the approving elder,
And finds his heart's desire, as we all do:
A wife, a chief; a mother and a father.
Prizes are given him, but he must strive
To test them countless times for certainty,
For assay. Can it be true? Can it be true?
Poems have promised him it would be true.

5. *At Twenty-Two. Cambridge.*

His Cambridge was the Cambridge of the poets—
Dawn on the river, fervency of friendship,
Young men striving. (Dream no more of dark houses.)
His editor and benefactor, Squire,
Cool as a father in his patronage,
Lent almost every pound he could afford
Whenever he remembered to enclose it.
Spurred on, the student edited, disputed,
Wrangled and charmed. ('Breakfast with Sidney Webb.'
'Sassoon and Arnold Bennett came to tea.')
He drenched himself in poetry that held
To English tunes. His poems sprang to paper

And into print. He grieved and swore and counted
The ways his love betrayed him, while his friends,
Ackerley, Kitto, Priestley, Campbell, Kendon,
Bound by the lavish loyalties of youth,
Stood by his midnights, heard out his laments,
Read him their poems in return for his.
He was, it was said, the perfect Cambridge poet.
No one at Cambridge carried so much poetry
Close to the surface, fresh and potable.
Sluicing and plunging through a hundred months
Of loves and labors, quarrels, debts and rages,
He squandered all the energy (he mourned
In later years) that should have served to carry
His poems out of luck and into truth.
After so ravening an orgy, fear
Of weariness would trouble him forever.

6.   *At Sixteen. South Shields.*

His mother sits alone in the narrow house
On a Tyneside street, waiting for the weekly
Cheque to arrive from the man the children knew
As Uncle Ted. The weeks it did not come
The milkman and the grocer gave her credit
Because she always spoke to them like a lady.
When did the boy first hear the sound of poems?
Not in the slums, the collieries and streets
Where draymen, coalmen, dustmen clumped and ranted.
Not in the South Shields Empire Theatre where jugglers,
Comics and pratfall people woke the dead
At ten performances a week while he
Sat in the darkness of the street outside,
A ticket-seller at fifteen. The following year
(Six inches yet to grow till he was grown)
He called himself eighteen and sought his fortune,
A place in Churchill's Royal Naval Division,
Setting to work on his self-education.
He sat in uniform and did the duty
For five years keeping records at the Crystal Palace.
Poetry came to him, beginning with Sophocles,

Tennyson (Everyman Library), Spenser, Shakespeare,
Lamb and Coleridge. Behind them all lay
The Church of England, where still the language of Cranmer
Rang like a bell. Lord, I am not worthy to sit at Thy table.
And, seasoning this, 'Woman, her power and charm'.

7. *His Rest, 1970. Massachusetts.*

Now life has blunted the edges of his fury.
Mistrals of laceration and self-betrayal
Wither his bloom, bring frost to the harvest of youth.
His childhood, trodden beneath an implacable boot,
Lies motionless as memory in water
Where bones lie scattered shellmeal on the bottom.
Stricken by years of labor and rancor, all
For little but a blessing by the fathers,
The poet dies. A creature dies with him
Who had long lost the way into his poems.
We never understood his shrieks of rage
Damning the multitude of mousy deaths
That, year by year, would parch him into silence—
A swollen body lying on a plank.
Surviving him, we carry the poet's flesh
Reduced to ashes in a canister
Along a path to the summit of a cliff
Where Indians used to hold their summer vigil
Over the shellfish marshes and the sea.
We let the bones and ashes tumble out,
Dusting the granite in their heavy fall
Until they catch and rest in crevices
Or sink dissolving in the tepid brack
Of marsh below. And now his thirsty body
Is part of the land at last, land of his children,
Where the gray ungiving stone can always stand
For fathers, thrusting up above the fields
Not ever his own, though dearer than the land
That gave him birth but never knew his name.

GROUND

This stuff is what we are born from. Before my eyes
and between my fingers—grainy, sticky, chalky—
the provisions lie at hand for life to burst out of.
How stubbornly it behaves, baked hard as biscuits
in summer, yet, thawed by spring, spreading wide
to swallow a hundred horses, and in winter
rigid enough to scrape knuckles and crack bones.
It would seem to yield no passage, except that roots
as delicate as hairs can pierce hardscrabble
without a bruise or blister and hold their course
whether opposed by gravel or mud. By tasting it,
farmers can guess at what may come of its favors,
whether their crops will require manure or limestone.
We savor in the first-plucked leaf of lettuce
the lingering fragrance of Sun, which slips away
with the soil that bestowed it almost within the hour,
just as fish lose their colors out of water . . .
as I would despair if you were dead.

STANDING FAST: FOX INTO HEDGEHOG

After these years of sniffing the air at hedges,
leaping so gingerly as to leave no footprints,
tiptoeing through streams to wash off my own scent,
and walking welcome at night into the houses of hens,
my paws grow clumsy; my spine curls into a hoop;
these claws must be given over to scrabbling and scuttling.

No more prancing. My snout, the air-taster,
now stiffens itself for rooting. The silken ears,
the blazing tail, the shimmering pelt, gather up
the color of gray earth. No more flight or pursuit.

Quarry for all comers, I crouch in furrows,
keep away from light, bristle at a footfall,
my body set up for surprise. Stand fast, here, now.
No call to run quick. I know what I know.

A VOICE IN THE MOUNTAIN

(*1977*)

And he said, Go forth, and stand upon the mount
before the Lord. And, behold, the Lord passed by,
and a great and strong wind rent the mountains, and
brake in pieces the rocks before the Lord; but the
Lord was not in the wind: and after the wind an
earthquake; but the Lord was not in the earthquake:
And after the earthquake a fire; but the Lord was
not in the fire: and after the fire a still small voice.
And it was so, when Elijah heard it, that he wrapped
his face in his mantle, and went out, and stood in the
entering in of the cave. And, behold, there came a
voice unto him, and said, What doest thou here, Elijah?

I KINGS: 19:11–13

FOR NATALIE WEINER DAVISON

(1899–1959)

Für die Zeit wo du g'liebt mi hast
Dank i dir schön,
Und i wünsch, das dirs anderswo
Besser mag gehn.

LYING IN THE SHADE (*After Trilussa*)

Reading, as usual, in The New Yorker,
behind a haystack, chewing on a straw,
I see a swine and say, "So long, old porker!"
I see an ass and say, "So long, hee-haw!"

Such beasts won't take my meaning very far
so I'll be satisfied if I can tell
a little of the way things really are
without the risk of ending in a cell.

ALL' OMBRA (Trilussa)

Mentre me leggo er solito giornale
Spaparacchiato all' ombra d'un pajaro
Vedo un porco e je dico:—Addio, majale!—
Vedo un ciuccio e je dico:—Addio, somaro!—

Forse 'ste bestie nun me capiranno,
Ma provo armeno la soddisfazione
De poté di le cose come stanno
Senza paura de finì in priggione.

CIRCOLO DELLA CACCIA

(For Douglas Allanbrook)

Italian butchers love the shooting season.
It lasts at least six months, some places longer.
Thrushes, larks, and other speckled singers
hang up to ripen, dangling by their bloody
beaks, eyes glassy, feather coats bedraggled.
Any old bird who makes it through the season
has lasted out a war—the hunters number
twice any army Italy has mustered—
imposing laws of natural selection
for songlessness or silence in the woods.
Just scuff your shoe on any gravel walk
and thickets are vacated on the instant
with a desperate scramble and a chirped alarm.
Then hours go by without a glimpse of a bird,
just distant songs of sex and altercations.
You wonder why the hunters never shoot
at swallows that patrol the city rivers
hell-bent as bats, or bag the swifts that twitter
above your head at cocktails on the terrace.
Though songbirds of open spaces, fields and mountains
are hunted down, fair game, to turn on spits
and freshen the mouth's appetite for wine,
I once for three acts watched a sparrow flutter
around an opera house's chandelier
while every eye was fixed upon Mimi
and no one noticed the bird until he dropped
dead on the stage abaft of the soprano.

ZENITH: WALKER CREEK

The woodcock now spends his evenings more quietly.
The robin sings less urgently, more chirpy.
Grass which sprang up for a while as though
it meant to reach the stars each afternoon
has moderated its ambitions a little.
The fields have settled down to heavy feeding and breeding.
Marsh, its winter khaki conquered,
has greened itself into equator color,
swaying taller and taller with the tides' tickling.
"Nature's first green is gold." Her second
is opaque as billiard tables. Now she plays her game,
less urgency in the dawns, less melodrama.
The pheasant's declaration rings out half as often;
the minnows flutter calmly in their pools,
having learned their prey cannot escape.
The shade is deeper, more desirable.
Dogs trot in preference to running,
spend more of daylight sprawling and panting.
The pedalling bicyclists shift to lower gears,
the bay blooms with looser and larger sails.
Our sun has given of its best in waxing:
It teeters above our heads as nearly
as the earth's escapism will permit,
toppling with some reluctance after noon
toward the West to keep us on the boil
till the anger of flies and the hunger of mosquitoes
drive us from sun to shade, from shade to the shelter
of screens, where, after fall of darkness, we drown
our senses in sunburn, poison ivy, gin.
Drinking deep, hot-headed, we sleep dark.
Those long days were the promises we broke.

BICENTENNIAL

The cinquefoil in the field
stands up to yellow clover,
strawberries, hawkweed,
daisies almost over.

Swallows dive and swoop;
they tremble, glide and roll.
Necklaces of wren-song
chatter down the stone wall.

Roses stud the edge of the woods
where goldenrod is growing.
Ovenbirds are teaching.
Cattle might be lowing

were trees not making motions
to wipe our fields away.
Two hundred years of farming?
A single stand of hay.

MAKING MUCH OF ORIOLES

Teetering high in the feathers of an elm,
two orioles chortled halfway into spring
while their green cover faded into dun,
breasting the normal current of the season.
The tree trunk bled wet life into the ground.
Dutch elm disease. The tree had been no beauty,
strangled in its early days by grapevine,
embraced by poison ivy, tickled by thistles;
yet when it was felled an unfamiliar light
erased familiar shadows from the garden.

I walked around the tree to count the branches
that must be lopped before the trunk could be
bucked into cordwood. Here, suspended sideways,
a pouch of gray silk dangled, gave out peeping.
Three chicks inside, as featherless and bright
as oranges, crouched back and yawned in my face.
Parental discord rang from nearby willows.

Maybe the nest could be removed, like houses
that block the highway, crawling on a trailer,
or bob behind a tugboat, buoyed and hawsered
betwixt the fishing villages of Newfoundland.
I pruned the dangling branch that held the nest
at its tip, like moss wrapped round a finger,
and cradled it along a ladder, stretched
as high up a chokecherry tree as I could reach,
fifty feet short of normal oriole altitude.
The chicks kept cheeping, fearful for their balance
when borne by clumsy hands and not the wind.
With every knot I wound another tie
between the elm branch and the cherry tree,
hanging the nest too high for predators.

Now for the parents, fixated on elms.
They hovered frantically near the supine tree
in search of the family they'd left dangling,
three chicks too small to fly, a nest

redoubtable enough to brave the elements.
How to believe that house could simply vanish
to rebuild in an unfamiliar tree?
I waited, sometimes whistling their calls,
a mocking-man who sang in dialect.
It might—or not—have been an accident
that before sundown the elders took their nest
at cherry value, unfamiliar height,
with chicks inside that must have been their own.
For several weeks I watched them come and go,
mother or father fetching food, while one
sang unto heaven in a higher tree.
The elm-leaves grew brown and dry and dead,
but twine still bound elm to the darker cherry
while, in the nest, the chicks gained flying weight.

One morning in July the nest was empty.
The younger and the older birds had gone:
parents and children roamed the world together.
The withered nest hung on, now limp, a trophy
of something like a victory of will.
I climbed the ladder to untie my knots
and hung the dried branch with its tattered flag
on the wall of my room, perhaps to hatch its meaning.

But a nest is no place to arrest a song
that in its very nature has no end.
The second year the orioles found an elm
to build in somewhere in the neighborhood.
They might have been my nestlings. I don't know.
I've tossed the branch behind a lilac bush.

DAY OF WRATH

September silence sags over the field.
Faded summer denims flap with fatigue
on a neighbor's clothesline.
No birds sing, only crickets and katydids.
Yesterday the heaven twittered with swallows;
today at noon the wires are swept empty
of occupants. From an enormous distance
the crow cries out his carrion comfort.
The pasture, lately mowed, noses aside yellow bristles
with a new cropspill of bluegreen autumn blades.
The sun sizzles on rocks, striking raisinly wrinkles
into the unpicked grapes, which white-tailed hornets
ignore, to feast on the drowsy flies
who do not hear them coming.
The marsh tides move like syrup.
Their dark water stirs the seed-heavy grasses
like masts of sloops at anchor.
Beechnut hulls bristle under the
toughening hats of their leafage.
Gardens have been harvested of beans and corn.
The dry soil flourishes mostly with immigrants:
brussels sprouts, broccoli, *aubergines, poireaux.*
Shortening days turn crisp after nightfall.
By day the air still hums with the sound of sleep.
This afternoon is tangled in its silence
until a yellow dog, posted to guard an empty house,
lets out a howl. His desertedness will never end.
No man will cross the road for his relief.
His work of watching will go on forever.

AUTUMN ZODIAC

(For J. B. Priestley at Eighty)

Autumn houses her faith in dreams of spring:
her toughened dusky petals hold till frost
the cells of sprigs that woke along the marl
before a mote of color starred the garden.
September roses keep their youth alive
till all the jonquils' fingerholds have sunk
deep into memory: could they have ever existed?

You often tease us into springtime dreams
of all the bright days that preceded this one,
such memories as time has laid to sleep,
roles in the play we all perform together,
seasons never forgotten though forgotten.
The years swim forward in your scenes and pages
to the dressing-room where each, wherever his seat,
must stare at the unfamiliar face of his mirror.
There the cold caustic of our century
has scarred the promises that we believed.
Yet Virgo smiles at us like every wife
who owes her harvest to unclouded spring.

CROSS CUT

Slumped on a pallet of winter-withered grass
you lie dead at my feet, in age not quite
a century, perhaps, but twice as old as I am,
in a pose your twisted trunk and dwindling leaves
had never hinted, even at your sickest.
How many stubs your gangrened upper branches
had turned into sockets and armpits
for squirrel, coon and starling
to burrow in! You thrust erect as stiff
as the memory of my oldest neighbor who watches
each new spring for your fluttering bloom
and every August for a pride of pears—
green to the eye, woody to the tooth,
taut and cidery to the fumbling tongue.
For years we've watched you dying from the top,
a peril to climbing children and seekers of shade,
but knew that, pear-like, you could stand for years,
heart eaten out, just fingering your life.
Perhaps I could have helped you out of the air
with some shreds of your stature left intact,
but now I've failed you. You lie invisible
behind the wall, your most disgraceful branches
lopped and hauled for firewood, resting scarred,
beyond your element, crushed by your own weight,
shapeless and pitiful as a beachbound whale.
Only inches above the nourishing ground
a cross-cut stump, stark white, reveals at bottom
you're still as lively as the day you bloomed.
The hearts of your leaves shone out in valentines
and your windborne, lilting, sinewy boughs
heaped proudly up toward the waning sun
those glowing, softly tinted, bumper bushels.

SKIING BY MOONLIGHT

Orion reclines on his hip.
Polaris glares high at my left.
I glide my way homeward,
a quarter-moon chasing me.

We follow the lurching shadow
of my sweaty body back
along the newly-crumbled tracks
I slogged only an hour ago

through the mirror-image pasture.
(Polaris twinkled at my right,
Orion teetered at my left;
the moon, narrow as a candle,

sparkled on smooth, blameless snow,
a beach of diamonds.
Cedars were heaped with treasure
among frozen cherry trees.)

Our sheep have all taken shelter
within the black barn.
In the windless moonlight
only an owl hoots against the cold

while deer, silent among pines,
wait to hear my skis stop hissing
and the back door click shut

before they wade toward the rick
to steal some hay.

THE HAWK OF THE MIND

No mind, no mind. What settles down around me
must not be left for the rain to wash away.
I need my mind, but no, it will not answer.
The maples are darkening in the August day.
The standing grass is drying into hay.
Swallows, fledged and grown, chatter in the sky
or warm themselves on the rooftree.
Their blood has not yet been spilled,
but the hawk of the mind is waiting.

HASKELL'S MILL

Legend foams up around this farmlike place
that looks both landward and toward the tides
whose surf is hammering behind the hill.
Tales are written of an abandoned gristmill,
"one of the first tidal mills in the New World,"
that cooled the heels of a hundred Union soldiers
parching in bivouac one summer day:
"Their captain marched them down to the creek
at high tide and off the mill dam, in columns."
It stood within eyeshot of this very house.
Almost a hundred years ago the mill
produced its final particle of flour.
With no compacted power in the waters
a mill's no better than a ruined city,
a pencil mark beside the illiterate tides.
Still, we remember. There's a little left
of Haskell's Mill, "the remains of the dam, some rocks
and waterlogged timbers." The Haskells had been given
"the license of the town in 1690
to build this tide mill for grinding corn.
The tide was high enough there, certainly,
to make a pool of every incoming tide.
The controlled outflow turned the water wheel.
Vessels are claimed to have docked here
to take on meal for the West Indies trade." *

Do we remember? The books remind us, and
beside the creek where boys still dig for worms
they all recall the spot as "Haskell's Mill."
A ruined skiff rots by the waterside.
The yellowlegs and plover scream in voices
anxious with autumn, with migration coming.
High tide pours in, kingfishers skim the pool,
crabs nibble at the rising of the tide,
and gulls search hopefully along the brink
only to flap away where fancy calls.
At the far end of a sloping stony track

* Joseph E. Garland, *The Gloucester Guide*, 1973

the shingled house of food stood by the water.
The center post, the thickness of a tree,
bore up the millstones, grooved and geared to grind
opposed, in and out of disengagement,
governed by pulleys and levers with hickory handles
to make the slab stones kiss and scour each other.
At every touch white flour puffed and drizzled
down through a funnel in the nether stone
to rise, like bleached sand in an hourglass,
until the hopper filled, and then the mealsacks,
and then the lighters shuttling to the ship
to weigh anchor, to set sail for the islands.

The millstones now lie buried in the ground,
doorsteps for the houses of two neighbors,
Parsons and Roberts, who had not been born
the day the stones cracked the last grain of wheat
and lapsed into disuse and passive silence.
The tide seizes and rattles fists of stone
at random. We've withdrawn allegiance
from land and sea. We take our pay from strangers,
unthinkable during the two hundred years
when Haskell's Mill encouraged every farmer
to drag his wagonload to the waterside.
The Mill served children as a diving platform
for the mill-pool's swimming hole, and then it was gone.
All the wheatfields that catered to its stones
are built up or grown over. The farms are woodland,
sprinkled with cars that have been left for dead
after carting city people to a country
where nothing is produced and little earned.
The neighbors marry, hold a job, and keep
their land in hopes developers will buy
to spare them the indignity of ruins.

Not even rumor can recall the miller,
the ruler of the cropland and the marsh,
a figure standing in a primal world
that planted crops and turned them into meal

without the use of any other force
than the human mind and nature in her seasons.
He served in an apron crusted stiff with flour
while water howled and millwheels groaned and trembled.
He held the balance between sea and land,
the sun and moon, the water and the stone.

THANKSGIVING

(For Gunilla Jainchill)

By the authority vested in me, a gift,
(in German, *poison*; in Swedish, a *marriage*)
I write of journeys, placenames, interventions,
inheritances visible, alive, dead.
A milkweed pod atop its autumn stalk
bulges from cold and flips itself wide open.
It sprinkles flurries of snow between the grassblades
to bloom, mulberry-like, for next midsummer,
nourished by milk no bitterer, no whiter
than any I have tasted as a gift.

THE FALL OF THE DOLLS' HOUSE

The family figurines sat round a fire
at the hearth of a dolls' house, porcelain-faced,
dove-breasted, leaning against each other,
smiling as though their rage were ruled by music,
the transcendental chords of Plato's dream.
Father, a kindly provider, judge, and priest,
Mother, a milkmaid, mending things, healing,
Children at play, at rest, reading their lessons—
such are the lessons that our lessons taught.
A window-frame hemmed in this perfect scene
for all to worship, as we worship icons.

Beside the dolls' house that the family built
the father's drunk. His wife weeps for her sex.
Young Tim is crippled and will surely die.
The older children dream of rape and murder,
for which of them has strength enough to act
as ancestor? The dolls' house shows them how
all parents fail, the Virgin fails the Child.
Their icon topples before war, change, chaos;
embraces yield to riots in the streets.
The pulse beats hard when Manson or Attila
kicks in the fire door, wrestles down Papá,
mugs mother, rapes the girl, snaps like twigs
the GI crutches of poor Tiny Tim.

Look at the dolls' house my grandparents owned
(its furniture imported from Saxe-Coburg)
in this contented photo. In another
the harmony of Diderot and Newton
takes on the dissonance of Marx and Freud.
My parents' glamor hints a naughty streak:
their dolls wear knickers, camisoles, bandeaux.
In a more recent snap, my wife and I,
nurtured on Tillich, Kierkegaard, Jung,
wear casual clothes but strike a mannered pose.
I slouch eccentric, while she smiles, protecting

the children underneath a cherry tree.
We'll leave the house, I think. The leaves are falling.

My children see themselves as in a poster:
unisex, well-provided, amplified.
Shatter the house, my darlings, helter-skelter!
The harmonies of our philosophy
have let us sleep through years of cuckoo-clocks
in drawing-rooms of matchsticks, cards, and lace.
If you are granted wishes for the world,
enlarge its scope: make work as one with play
in houses built for everlasting fire
where man and woman burn like seraphim.

OFFISSA POPP

A Maneuver in Class Warfare

My father suited up
for two world wars
but was never recruited
to clean a weapon:
officer material.
Between wars he fancied
firing a borrowed shotgun
at (or near) birds.
But once a pheasant
whom he had stunned
and left me to carry
came undone.
Father strode on
gunning and missing.
His bird woke up
and stared me down.
The two of us sat
in the stubbled cornfield.
That was that.

One war later
he took up skeet.
His pals at the range
kept his twelve-gauge shiny;
but when he made
his big move to town
the gun was cleaned,
packed up, broke down.

A third war came
along, and I
went off to do
my hitch—G.I.
On my discharge
my father pleaded
he badly needed
his shotgun cleaned.

He needed it now
but he didn't know how.
As a boy whose mother
had never let him bother
with guns or other
store-bought mayhem,
I wondered why
a former G.I.
should serve this two-time fat man
as a batman?

Duty scoured the Winchester
with patches and rods.
Apologizing to the gods
of war, I poured,
and smeared the pad
with olive oil
(nothing else on hand)
and scrubbed out the gun
in pride and pity,
preserving the citi-
zens' right to bear
arms, by hiding a piece
like an adulterer's underwear
behind the galoshes
in a sixteenth-floor closet
on Fifty-seventh Street
in New York City.

Oh I polished the gun
he thought he might flourish
but he never assembled it
before he passed on.
When his executor
sold it for a pittance,
it was lubricated all right.
The bore shone bright.
An enlisted man's fate
is to clean his gun

before he may eat.
I should have beat-
en the thing into
a goddam plowshare.

HOUSE HOLDING

(For Carleton Coon and Peter Blake, who have never met.)

> *Except the Lord build the house, they labor in vain
> that build it; except the Lord keep the city, the watch-
> man waketh but in vain.*
> *It is vain for you to rise up early, to sit up late, to eat
> the bread of sorrows; for so He giveth his beloved sleep.*
> PSALM 127

THE NEW WORLD

They came to America to seek their "fortune"
(in other words, some land to build a house).
As immigrants they always talked of *home*,
called themselves *homebodies, homeward bound,*
were verbed by houses—*housed, housebound, housewarming.*
Thoreau, most virginal of men, inveighed
at snails weighed down by barns upon their backs.
Strip off, he said, and take yourselves to the woods.
The woods grew gloomy with disfranchised men
whose barns sagged down on them and wives despaired,
their children stunted. Cattle died. Game
grew scarce in field and woodland. Backyards
filled up with crippled and corroding Plymouths.
They shut the house and looked for work in the city.
Their sons went off in wartime to defend
whatever everyone had meant by *home*.
On upland acres, tottering granite walls
wander forgotten through a maple forest
to disappear in beaver-ponds and swamp.
Clearings crowd in upon old cellar-holes
marked by a lilac clump or rambler rose.
The country, though it emptied into town,
kept hold upon the brave, the poor, the haunted.
Transplanted sons bought up abandoned farms
to travel miles and miles to reach a house
they'd use to rest their bodies from the journey.
Overgrown hayfields and logging roads
have been spruced up with knotty-pine chalets
built *pour le sport* and locked up out of season.

161

Wild snowmobiles arrive on winter nights
to howl an hour or so, leave a window smashed,
allowing birds and beasts to enter in
and breed a second generation of ruin.

HOUSING STARTS

Most animals have no houses, only holes
to sleep and breed and shut things out. Held in
on themselves by scales, shells, feathers, fur,
reflexes, instinct, most of all a surer
sense of their senses, bodies are their houses.
Man's models for the house are nests and keeps.
(Most women tend to think of it as nest.)
A house has "many mansions." It is built
on sand or on a rock. A house is haunted.
A child thinks of his house as being his
before he thinks of land as being his.
Sometimes the house is made of cake. Sometimes
it's a high castle with a hedge of thorns,
or else a cosy cottage in the woods
with milk and strawberries on a wooden table.

ELEVATIONS

As citizens we seal ourselves in cells.
Thanks to our furnaces, pumps and wires,
each family has its fixtures. Even dogs
have private kennels, which their masters share.
When tenants meet in halls or elevators
they have no space or leisure to display
whether they're bent on hunger or on war.
They offer grins that are uneasy mixtures.
Each Living Unit stands upon the walls
of one beneath, shouldering one above.
Those who have no names, who share a wall with us,
we hear them and we hate them all. We know
six families live their lives beneath our carpet
(six more beneath our neighbor's and his neighbor's).

We have collected into humming hives
chiefly for profit. Nothing is collective
but passages for entry or for voiding.
Each couple makes its bed within a cube
to make of it a poem or a grave—
or just enough of each to found a family.

THE RADIANT CITY

Thus with concrete and shining steel new men
have taught us to employ clean catalogues
to plan our houses. Public law defends
their right to build, a right we have disused
along with other arts we have forgotten.
We camp outside until the men have finished,
and only then move in and leave the women
to settle our prefabricated chairs
and pets and pictures. Men make easy exits.
They leave their charming women to endure
in men-built houses, in their mastered lives.
Once they have settled in the frightened suburb,
wives dedicate their houses to the night,
absent themselves by day. Till recently
they had not known escape unless by force
or poverty, to factories or mines,
theatres or brothels, likely marriages.
Now they move boldly, yearn to be more manly.

In high-rise offices the males agree
that our republic's democratic creed
requires a house for feeding in and sleeping.
"New housing is a crying social need."
Men assume positions where they can
cover with walls their women's nakedness
and rear in children visions for a man.
Housing in quantity expels distress.
Why then, returning home at night, do we
find women cursing and our children weeping?

LA CATHÉDRALE ENGLOUTIE

An ancient place. The roofs are high and grey.
A friend and I walk down a cobbled street.
I've never seen an alleyway so neat:
brisk brooms have swept each speck of dust away.

No motor, tire or wheel makes hiss or clatter
across the squares or past the whitewashed angles.
My friend says, "poor and rich agree: no wrangles!
Here nothing has ever seemed to be the matter."

In the cathedral square the Church stands fast:
its leaded panes of red and blue depict
a squad of sturdy saints, with spires erect
unsmirched by soot or by iconoclast.

Within, black hats and furled umbrellas press
past chapels of mahogany, toward cages
that stand behind the apse, to bank their wages
and scribble checks where sinners once confessed.

Observe the great south aisle, the Bishop's Tomb:
walk out into the nave. No monk or priest
makes antiphon, and no one kneels. From east
to west a flock of tables fills the room,

and banqueters participate in revel.
They dance and drink from foamy steins of beer
between the speeches. How they love to hear
that cash has saved the country from the devil!

"Listen, my friend, what made your family chafe
to live in any other town? Why here?"
We walk in silence through another square.
"The schools are good," he sighs. "The streets are safe."

THE HANGING MAN

Hoist by an ankle,
my every joint squeaks.
Hair hangs from my head
as though scared to death.
I am held to the globe
by anti-gravity.
Pigs and chickens, however,
stroll past on the ceiling
apparently none the worse.

One gets used to anything.
Water runs uphill,
clouds rub their backs on the floor,
sunshine leaks its way
up through a hole in the ground.
Despite my excitable hair
I look introverted
(so upright friends tell me):
an arm and leg akimbo,
the ankle below the right foot
structurally startling.

A world like this
(Was there another?)
sets me tip-top,
hangdog, invert,
slewfoot, periculous.
I sway with each breeze
that whistles past my foot
and peep at overhead pebbles
whirling like hail;

but I see what the pigs
and chickens cannot see:
a world running down
despite all appearances.
Tolerating this anti-world
has made me the only
joke in the deck.
My only hope
is to be dealt with
or cut down.

THE COMPOUND EYE

(For L. E. Sissman, 1928–1976)

What an intolerable deal of history!
You were the fly upon a thousand walls,
the poet's eye with many hundred lenses,
master of every curiosity.
Marked down for death, nipped early at the heels,
you walked with shambling evasion, not in a hurry,
too proud to betray the merest smudge of panic.
Yet in your poems death lies never far
from the surface, knife beneath the water,
dark age pending. To stay alive for it
tubers and relics of each season's growth
must be tucked into order, time, and place.
Familiar phrases bowed beneath strange burdens
("a pleasure dome of Klees and Watteaus made"),
pleasures of a couplet coupled with
the nausea of chemotherapy.
Amid the disorder of illness, dying, death,
you put in order your arrested life.

Go, prince: peer owlish through the windowpane
betwixt the daintiness of your imagination
and all the tawdriness and disarray
our life is dressed in. From the postwar city
look out at the city of God, and then confess
how sweet was the disorder in the dress.

TOWARD AN UNDERSTANDING OF
THE PUBLIC LIFE

The President, my father, and myself
drove out along Route 6. Dog came for the ride.
The President had just resigned. Father was some years dead.
The President was clearly loth
to attract public notice. No one in the car
except for Dog had much to say to Nixon,
but otherwise we travelled pretty easy.
In mid-Cape Cod a tire blew out. The Pres-
ident was amazed, for in High Office such
things hardly ever happen. He refused to dismount.
Nothing for me but to hoof it, lugging a three-gallon can.
I found no filling-stations open (the roads
were crowded with traffic attending Gaudí cathedrals)
but I did locate a garage, sited where two one-way
streets began: where cars might leave but not enter.
Our options exhausted, we abandoned the car
and checked ourselves into a small hotel
where tongue-and-groove planks line the corridor,
floors dark with rust-and-green linoleum.
Here we lodge to this day: my father dead and silent,
Dog an unregistered guest. I observe
and record the President's words. He paces his room
insisting on his innocence and our guilt.

THE POEM IN THE PARK

She waited eagerly on a park bench,
holding in her arms the humming of the day,
her eyes welling with *lacrimae rerum*.
I walked toward her through the bricky streets,
tasting as I came the sky of the public park,
its gates ajar, its paths cast wide in welcome,
the bench warm beside her
with the words the poem and I would engage together.
But as I walked in under the sighing trees,
a gust of wind scattered from the dark pond
a flock of mallards, wings whistling,
crying out and fanning toward the harbor
over the buildings between the park and the sea.

Not till hours later, hemmed in between
office telephone and office typewriter,
did it come back to me. I'd left the poem
seated motionless upon a wooden bench
with tears in its eyes.

LA BOCCA DELLA VERITÀ

*The little piazza called the Mouth of Truth after the
big marble face of the sun in the church portico, whose
mouth was supposed to snap shut if you put your hand
in it and told a lie, but which was perhaps an ancient
sewer lid . . .* ELEANOR CLARK, *Rome and a Villa*

I thrust my fingers, crossed in an artful lie,
into the mouth of truth, the fluid of sex,
the darkness of death, murmuring tuneful noises.
The porch of a church ought to be good for a gamble.
In front, the face of the sun. Behind, the temples,
one round, Tempio di Vesta, home and hearth,
one square, Tempio della Fortuna Virile.
Both sexes call on us to tell the truth.

If I speak out, will doves and bluebirds descend
and the butterflies of the world slip their leashes?
If I tell, will tigers carry me to Tibet
or elect me poet-priest of a sunlit island?
I have turned away from the pleaders
and pretended to be asleep.
Only a stone's throw from Cloaca Maxima
I cringe in the lap of the great goddess,
shrinking from these monumental Roman exertions.
Who asked my soul to magnify the Lord?

Take the right hand. Place it in the sun's mouth.
If art is not "a lie that tells the truth,"
why else, except in aid of some good God,
should I hope to tell the world my kind of lie
and not be swallowed by a river of darkness?

I dare to pledge my powers to the sun.
How coldly will the marble give its answer?
If I have truly lied in the mouth of truth
let my right hand forget her cunning.

HEAD STONE

The great rock blazes high above the marsh.
From its highest foothold my father's ashes were scattered.
Much lordlier than any human chieftain,
the cliff allows high tides to lick its foot
and gathers pines around it like a blanket.
When I'm asleep, as well be dead as absent
from weather and the rock. The trees, unpruned,
squeeze out new shoots despite all seasons' endings.
The compost seethes beneath its quilt of straw.
In the autumn, sun springs up in the grass but freezes,
halted by dark winds jostling from the mountains
to kindle maple, sumac, beech and oak
into cold standards gorged erect with flame.
The land is all I'm given to imagine.
In absences I might as well be dead,
a vole's trig corpse beneath the currant bushes.
What goes on, gone? Friends die. Some few of them
dispatch themselves. It happens in their rooms
and books, in blankets, in their buried beds,
the bedrock of their basements, in their graves.
The rock, in presence or in absence, glows
like old love letters. It endures, no matter,
when no more dreams are stirring on the farm
and no true feeling leaves no memory.

CREATURES OF THE GENITIVE

(For Frances Lindley)

Adjectives of desire, knowledge, memory, power,
fullness, sharing, and guilt take the genitive.
RULE OF LATIN GRAMMAR

Something lay hidden deep within the mountain.
I don't know what. Perhaps it could be love,
although I heard reports that thirsty tigers
had skulked around the heights in search of water
and startled tourists, full of food and wine,
exciting fear and other kinds of tension.

No wonder dreams like mine gave rise to tension
beyond whatever talk one heard of tigers.
What the high country left me with was love.
It followed me to settle near salt water,
but dreams went on for years beneath the mountain,
and memories as dizzying as wine.

The palate seldom has enough of wine,
but excess of indulgence heightens tension
so that your thirst transcends the power of love
to slake, a guilt as terrible as tigers.
A hundred strolls around our homely mountain
in quest, in endless quest, of crystal water

(O how dry country troubles you with water!)
brought me up short, or face to face with tigers
near brooks or lakes half up (or down) the mountain.
I tell you, I have had my share of tension.
Beneath the heights where all the world drinks wine,
two can afford the luxury of love.

One's second guess would have to be that love,
a thing as precious as untasted wine,
whether it wear the form of rocky mountains
or the transparent coverlet of tension,
is what the heart seeks when it desireth water.
But try to tell that to a thirsty tiger.

173

The hunger of the soul's a dream of tigers
mauling and snarling. Blunt their fangs with wine,
kiss knowledge in a whirlwind, crawl toward water,
trifle with fire and earthquake, piss on love,
lose nerve in each entanglement with tension—
and still a small voice murmurs in the mountain.

    Though memory tenses with the guilt of tigers,
    knowledge, desire, and love share sweetest water
    when the strong mountain fills itself with wine.

BARN FEVER AND OTHER POEMS

(*1981*)

GIFT: The act, right, or power of giving. *Webster*

Some quality or endowment given to man by
God or a deity. *Webster*

With respect to real estate, formerly, any
form of alienation. *Webster*

Something given to corrupt. A bribe.
Oxford

(German) Poison, toxin, virus, venom;
virulence, malice, fury. *Cassell's German
Dictionary*

(Swedish) Marriage

A gift in anticipation of impending death
is revocable until the death of the
giver, and then becomes absolute. *Webster*

FOR JANE, WRITING

For over twenty years you have endowed me
with poems it seemed to me I had discovered
and with nearly every stability
I knew enough to know.
Your laughter freckles the horizon,
aurora meridionalis.
You sit in a work chair
the way a heron stands—
motionless, gazing down at the paper.
Then, with the flicker of a smile,
you lean for the fish
with pencil or stammering key.

THE RAM BENEATH THE BARN

Deep in the dark beneath foundation walls
the thick ram lies, his bent forefeet tucked under.

The droppings of a winter foul his straw,
but I dare no longer venture to his level
with grain, hay, water. I lower them to him
as to a tribe closed off by mountain snows.

He walks out into the sun, looks up at me,
his eyes expressionless as agates. He waits
for the moment of revenge. One day he may
catch me in a corner! Meanwhile, to prime his aim,
he taps his head and horns against the granite.

Of course when autumn comes he will again
curl up his lips into the sneer of lust
and leap his docile ewes, rolling their stupid
eyes as he does them his service—

but in this March we stare each other down,
two rams caught in a thicket by the horns.

INTERVAL

In the thick air of early September
mornings, crows call uninterrupted,
no competition. The whirr of katydids
keeps up an incessant thermograph
of sound, invisible orchestra
rising with light and heat,
falling with cold and dark
to steal the place of songbirds in the spectrum.

In the trees squirrels scramble
to stuff their pouches
with a season of beech nuts.
In the garden they shinny
up sunflower stalks to keep
the black seeds from falling prey
to incoming winter birds.
Tomatoes enrich their sagging vines
like Christmas baubles.

Except for one abandoned chick
too slow or small to fly, lying broken
and dead beside the lawnmower,
the barn has emptied of swallows.

New piglets, just learning
the taste of man's food, skitter
away from the fence each time
a wagging dog approaches.
Geese roost in the shade.
Sheep munch stolidly whatever
green blades survive
as members of the yellow medley of grass.

On such days between
their summer jobs and school
the children sleep till noon,
clothes and towels swathing
the floor like serpents.

In the meadow a girl exercises
a long-barreled grey gelding
with patches on his rump
and a tail like a chieftain's whisk.
They canter together around and around the field.
Katydids lower their buzz.

Black leaves are scarcely moving
on the trees. Along the wires
and in the willow branches
a thousand tree swallows stir and twitter,
awaiting a signal
to set off for Yucatán.

LAMBKILL

(Sheep Laurel, kalmia angustifolia)

Yielding far more than we had ever sown—
lushness of fescue laced with grapevine
and poison ivy, raspberries loud with bees—
the land flowed with milkweed and honeysuckle
in surpluses that seemed to call for forage
by expansionist sheep. They had already munched
three pastures down to rugs. We felled and set
five dozen posts, strung a furlong of wire,
and set up gates to keep the sheep shut in.

At first they didn't like this newest pasture,
something about the wind, the angle of the sun,
marsh flies buzzing around their flipflop ears.
They slept burrowing their muzzles under each other.
Waking, they browsed their way through the inscrutable,
bawling out their wish for a view of level grass,
hungry for simplicity. They thrust heads
through the wiring of their fence to nibble lawn
that stretched out ahead like understanding
while cryptic stands of fodder rustled behind.

After three weeks of grazing, the meadow showed signs
of altering into pasture. The high grass dwindled.
Raspberries receded, poison ivy vanished.
Sheep trails stole a march across the ground.
We'd wondered whether a mere dozen animals
could clear out half an acre in a month,
and by the end of June it was nearly done.
On Sunday morning when I brought their grain
all but one sheep ran up at the clank
of the feeding pail. He, a five-month's ram,
stood oddly, head hanging, clearly sick.
An hour later he lay thrashing on his side
spasmodic by the galvanized water tub.
One ear had dropped askew beside one eye
that rolled askew. "It's got into his brain.

Don't treat him rough or he'll go into convulsions,"
the veterinarian said, jabbing him with a needle.

Riding home in the truck the lamb stood gamely
as though facing down a ring of predators,
but he fell when the truck jittered over a pothole
and could not rise. We laid him in a stall
on a mattress of hay, watching him sink and groan
in spite of all attention. We poured water
down his soft throat from a Barbaresco bottle,
stuffed him with purges to push through the poison
that he had gobbled somewhere in the field.
We listened like nurses to his gurgled breath,
laying hands on his hot shaggy flanks, wondering
whether we had left anything undone
we might have done, aghast at being "fastened to
a dying animal." We had no gift
to heal the staggered lamb who had used himself
to help us even out a straggling meadow.
He gave us back his breath in an exchange
for what the meadow gave him, sprigs of laurel
that had lurked deadly in the undergrowth
and plucked his tongue, his brain, among the roses.

BARN FEVER

Nobody knows how much to make of barns,
certainly not a barn as old as this,
set in a farm too swampy and too rocky
to make you rich by cutting hay or grazing.
Our barn was built two hundred years ago—
the lower half. The beams are as old as that.
It probably held harness, kept a horse,
provided cover for a wagon or a pung
and, with boards laid across its crooked roofbeams,
gave half its upper spaces up to hay.
That was before the old house tumbled down
late in the eighteen-fifties. Its next owner,
Malachi* Andrews, who was much involved
in swapping land, begetting farmer's children,
or buying boats for sons who'd rather fish,
rebuilt the barn and then the house and buildings.

That was the golden age of barns. Three farms
were merged by Malachi into a hundred acres
of upland, stoneland, woodland, all to pasture,
mostly for cows. The new half of the barn
stood high enough for storing up salt hay
and sheltering ten milk cows underneath
in wooden stalls so expertly designed,
fitted and whitewashed, that the cow's manure
could be scraped out, without shifting a hoof,
to flow into a cave in the foundations.
The new house, proportioned like the new barn,
rested on masonry as crisp and solid
as the barn's own blocks of fitted Cape Ann stone.
Next to the barn old Malachi then built,
on slender granite pillars that held it off
the ground, a corncrib with dovetailed corners,
and, near the house, a root cellar and milkshed
to keep the milk and fresh churned butter cool.

* The Gloucestermen pronounced it "Mellicky."

For fifty years the barn stood at the center
of the traffic of the farm, above the house
to screen it from the wind. Malachi Andrews,
his offspring scattering from Essex to Salem,
kept up his walls to keep his cows from scattering,
bought lots for firewood, orchard, maple sugar,
and drove to Gloucester every market day.
At night the cows swallowed their cud in the barn.
When Malachi died Elizabeth soon followed.
Their sons went off to sea or to New Jersey,
and two of his daughters, one of them once married,
kept up the barn for two cows and some hens
with only twelve acres left them of the hundred.
They hired a man to help them cut their hay
in the salt marsh and float it up by dory.
They let the sparse old pastureland revert
to meadow. Crab apple and swamp maple
began to creep into the fields which once
had been held open by the force of farming.
One day the two old women, clearing brush,
started a fire to burn the slash, and one,
Miss Mary Brown, was not quite quick enough
to keep her long skirt out of the teeth of the flames
which caught her, brought her down. Her sister
lived on in the house a while but sold the cows.

In the thirty years that passed before I came
trees nudged in and advanced upon the barn.
The corncrib rotted and fell, the milk shed collapsed.
The hayloft in the barn, no longer needed
to keep the cattle fed, was subdivided
by two flimsy floors and turned into
a battery for hens, and the cattle stanchions
were strung with chicken wire. No repairs.
Two years more, and the chicken farmer's busted.

The house passed to a Harvard anthropologist
who built himself bookcases in a parlor
that up to then had been reserved for funerals.
He fitted out the kitchen with an electric stove,

dug in new plants around the house, and set
his mind to keeping up a large green lawn—
sure sign that the barn had now become
poor second to a house that was no more a farmhouse.
The anthropologist who tamed the grass
decided the country had become too tame
and sold the farmland to a State Street lawyer
who feared the devastation that would come
if some bad bolshevik laid nuclear waste to Boston.
His wife wallpapered in anticipation.

My first view of the farm: a day in March,
walking with friends down the field between dry stalks.
The barn's soaked black with last night's rain. Its south
wall gapes black with apertures, its eaves are piebald
with doors of nests for squirrels. The high roof,
shingled with asphalt by the chicken farmer,
has lost a number of its links, as though
the wind had tried to scale it like a fish.
Inside, someone's Mercedes. On a beam
two cooing pigeons have scuffled together
a shaggy nest in case of warmer times
for breeding, hatching. All around the barn
sumac and other thicketry are shoving
against the base of the walls, as though to nudge
the ancient building off its pins. The barn
has no friends left, it seems. Some boys have smashed
the floorboards upstairs where the chickens roosted.
If I'm to own it, how to heal the barn?

The house had been infected by the suburbs.
I heard the barn beside it heave a sigh
anticipating usufruct; or else decline,
decay, a sagging and senility;
or, worse, more merciless, a careless match
to send it up in flames like Mary Brown.
Nobody knows how much to make of barns
that do not shelter anything we value.
The crops are spent that went to Haskell's Mill.
This land has turned too sour even for hay

and lies now unprotected by the walls
that run and stumble, madmen, through the woods
which no one cuts or culls. Why are our barns,
that do not shelter anything we value,
left standing as an emblem of a past
when we owned things we thought more worth the keeping?
Sometimes in summertime our younger children
may hide and seek here to remember games
their great-grandparents used to play in barns—
but Malachi and Mary Brown did more than play.
They metamorphosed grass into milk and butter,
kernels and clamshells into hens and eggs,
dead seeds into the brightness of beans and corn.
Somehow the barn is all that they have left us.
What else is lingering on the land to press
its bristling, fading harvests in our arms?
The smells of milk, manure, and straw, a life
beyond the games suburban children play?
Time and some care have spared this barn, a sign
of the work a farm does to keep itself a farm.
Without the barn there would be little cause
to call this piece of land more than a piece
of land, one corner of it fastened down
by a yellow house where people sit and write
about the days when the farm had farmers on it
as well as the busiest barn for miles around.

SATAN IN GOATSKIN

Disarmed on the unhandy
side of the wall, I note
the stern end of the goat
whose forward mouth rips off
my unpicked brussels sprouts.
Lobbed rocks, berserker shouts
shock a stark staring goat into
thick-bodied parody of deer
with grace abounding,
vaulting and clearing
the fence. After which Nanny,
mistress of double-agentry,
bowing, browsing,
shifts shape from pestered
fugitive to pastured
livestock, safely sealed in by wire
with sheep unsafely grazing.
O goat, teetering
on manly hindquarters!
Mount up upon that rock!
O nibble, happy and murderous,
sweet sprigs of apple.
O girdle the boughs.
O kill the tree forever.
O ass-end to our house,
flip up your tail
like the flap of a pocket
and salute the master
who fenced you in his pasture.

FAWN

(for Sam and Jessica Warren)

Late summer dusk. Headlights along the road.
A sudden apparition by the hedge.
My car swerved aside of its own wish,
an instep arch crushed on the brake pedal,
and stopped in an instant. Jumped out
to learn whether we had killed anything
without a sound or click of contact.
Lying on asphalt, dazed but conscious,
half-lay a spotted fawn, so scrawny that
I could not tell whether it had been struck
by hunger, illness, or accident. Over one eye
a slight cut, slightly bleeding. The fawn
blinked, lay still. Now other cars were halting.
Occupants were out, shouting advice.
The fawn reclined, dreamy and indifferent.
After a quarter hour of altercation
we heaved the passive, lally-legged baby
into a van, one of us holding a head
that did not need the holding, wary of
the hooves that did not move or strike,
and settled it inside a neighbor's barn
with a sheep-nipple, evaporated milk,
chlorate of lime, a bottle, barley-sugar.
Out of all these warm deer-milk was concocted
and fed into the fawn with deep resistance
from one so weak, so wild, so uncomplaining.
Blowing into the corner of her mouth
triggered a reflex that would make her suckle
and take enough to help her stay alive:
most of the milk ran down along her neck
but some was kept. She lay with folded legs
unmoving, making no attempt to rise
when her feeders approached, not attempting
to give more than a sniff of cooperation.
The second day we took her from the barn
and fed her on the lawn. Her keeper let her go,
and suddenly she found her feet, making for open

country, so weak she could not navigate,
staggering sideways, legs scissoring.
Now, when we tried to put her in the barn,
she flailed out at us with those edged hooves
and struggled till we feared not for ourselves
but her, that she might shatter against the wall.
The third and fourth days she was so much stronger
that her tail flicked up and down when she was fed,
and she clattered back and forth in the dark stall.
We took her carefully into the sun,
fed her one last bottle, stood up and back,
and let her go. She walked, mincing forward,
then broke into a trot, and as we watched
she cantered down the lawn and onto the marsh,
tail held high, then out of view into the alders
that border on the marsh. There is no knowing
if she survived the winter, but it was a mild one.

JULY MEETING

Crow hollered, barking darkness like a trumpet.
Mockingbird followed, dragging behind
a ragbag of moonlit virtuosity.
Robin, at the shank end of mating season,
purled and knit the customary declarations.
Other "feathered songsters" waited,
treading air to hold position
till the loudest at length stood aside.
The cardinal's whistle faded.
Dawn song broke down
into twitter of sparrow and wren,
dove's coo, the receding
ball-peen strokes of oven-bird,
catbird's stuttering clauses.
Finally, after each
had said his grey say,
sun sprang from the edge of sky
into a vacuum of sound,
rewarding every ruddy tree,
calling the world to order.

THATCH

(Spartina alterniflora)

Thatch uncrouches
from the thick brown mat
of marsh like stubble
from the planet's beard,
edges to the seaward side
of its self-humbling cousin
spartina patens,
flourishes seeds overhead
at blade's length, and
flicks them free
into a tide as salt as tears.

PARADISE AS A GARDEN

(For Elizabeth B. Moynihan)

One of the great tautologies: self-regarding:
in which the seeds of growth
are the kernels of contemplation,
in which the contemplation of desire
ekes out desire's last sigh,
in which what enlarges the space
is its surrounding hedges:
husk and flower are one.

These were no northern sprawls, however,
no meadows of bluets and flax.
In Persia water collected itself, at whatever
cost, within walls: model of a house or city:
no water, no life. Yet sometimes paradise
persisted as boundaries only, and in the end
the garden stood, bracelets of stone and water,
without leaf, flower, or fruit to carry temptation.

And so it follows, through ages, crosses and tongues,
that when we speak of our eternal delight,
whether a garden we were once expelled from
or one that has been lost and overgrown,
it is the edges we cannot forget.
Whatever persists within, forever fresh,
is the indelible border of imagination.

THE SOUND OF WINGS

1. *Present Air*

Snow falls off the roof with the sound of wings.
The clouds scud west to east across the sky.
Black birds, my life, starlings, jays and crows,
perch in the tapered boughs of silver trees
waiting for something to live or die. With wings
they barter inklings of life among themselves.

2. *Imperfect Water*

The tide creek fell the way the sun was climbing:
two hours of height until the tide struck low,
two hours till noon. Four hours since snow stopped feeding
the waters while they turned. Their latest high mark smeared
mud-brown against the crystal sheet of snow
while last year's fallen, near-forgotten grasses,
green all washed out by scores of scouring tides,
glared upward, ochre staining sea and sky.

3. *Perfect Fire*

The trees endowed us with this woodpile. Cherry, pear,
maple, and oak (with now and then a whiff
of cedar) have unlimbered, tottered,
and tumbled to the music of the saw,
have stacked their jackstraw limbs beside the barn,
mislaid their growth, fumbled their sap. Thus all
disordered fiber has been realigned
till flame shall filter out the hard from soft
and breathe its distillation to the air.

4. *Future Earth*

This will have been the season's virgin snow,
erasing every blemish, every landmark,
magnifying the earth and all therein
    while it shall continue.

Whether the sun will singe its lap-robe white
or water strip it naked to the air
or wind tuck snow high up against its shoulder,
    it will surely continue.

Its trees will spill their burdens to the wind
and tides will shear off fragments for the sea:
yet snow falls off the roof with the sound of wings
    and it shall continue.

ATMOSPHERES

(For Reg Saner)

1. *Boulder 1935*

Where the mountains lift from the plain
one of my boyhoods was toughened
in a stucco house, protected
by a palisade of lilacs,
purple one day in April,
the next bowed down in snow
that, melting, would uncover
red slate sidewalks
scribbled over with demotic
marks from children's rollerskates.

The snowflake came and went
in sparse Colorado air
that cracked the boards of pianos,
cooked eggs in cool water,
lifted cakes crankily,
stole away breath at hilltops,
and blotted stray moisture.

Oases? In one direction
the damp innards of Hanselman's
Greenhouse flaunted rainfall
orchids dangling from their roots.
In the other, the English throwback
of Mabel Reynolds' garden.
She watered it, ramrod straight,
enunciating consonants like musketry
to repel the elisions of the West,
while her husband, Shakespearian George,
smiled on the world as though it were a theatre.

The surfaced streets held hard.
Air sizzled in the lungs.
Rocks and gravel abraded
a boy's bare knees despite

the vapors of campus life,
the cries of football crowds
that cheered for Whizzer White,
the oohs and aahs of tourists
at how the falling light
carved shadows in the cliffs
that westward and high upward
clamped down an early sunset
on days that seldom darkened
except with stormclouds or dust
that blew west from the poisoned plains.

2.   *Cheyenne Mountain 1944*

Ten boys of sixteen roped up
on a red crumbling cliff,
guided by a trigonometry teacher.
Climbing boots scuffed the rock,
catching enough edge to heave
bodies over the lip
of a squat ledge, each of us
breathing deep catches of air.
There! Stopped. There, there!
Above, just above. Clear eyes,
moonlit glass, nostrilly head
carrying a sweeping spiral
of horn—stock still, steady
as the rock whose arm he stood on,
a wild ram, bighorn!
Motion and sound both ceased.
When breathing again began
and with a sudden snort,
one of the boys snatched up
his geologist's pick. On wire thighs
he charged the ram. Who blinked,
breathed himself across the outcrops,
seesawed silently upward
and was inhaled by the landscape.
Our pursuer had to halt,
blinking through fogged glasses.

Now decades later, Gifford is dead,
and only a cramped gathering of bighorns
clusters above timberline.

3. *National Center for Atmospheric Research 1967*

The fortieth parallel flies around the world
as though launched from the ramparts
of I.M. Pei's mind-fortress. My first guide
to the site, an ancient mathematician,
limped through portals whose lintels
of ground-up mountain stone
glittered slightly with mica.
Below the mesa where the Center stands,
down there in the little city of the plain
where my flesh had flowered for women,
the air drooped thick with pollutants.
The old mathematician croaked out the terrible force
of the geometric progression. "There is no escape.
Population expands, stark as compound interest.
A penny invested by Caesar at simple interest
would be worth a few thousand today; but a penny
at compound interest earns gold
as massive as the planet."
Ieoh Ming's palatial Chinese puzzle
sprouts from the flank of the foothill
like a dusty mushroom. Doorways shackle
vistas of the plains, unimpeded sights
of the sky, green-robed, pink-tinted mountains.
Glass in the windows is tinted
just enough to admit
all elements of the light except glare,
brilliance without dazzle.
Under the molded cover of the walls
unearthly silicon chips,
linked into computer circuits,
monitor the winds of the world
while at their side sit men and women
lightly breathing. Their house

of inquiry shelters without surprise
the earth's commotion, while
the chinook breathes warmly
on dissolving snow.

4. *Boulder 1979*

Where the mountains lift from the plain
I work beside a woman
in kerchief and rounded apron.
We extricate earthenware
from the racks of her kiln.
Her dishes, once moist clay,
now cool and hard as agate,
open their rough-scalloped
rims skyward to swallow
whatever happens to be served
on their surfaces. Flakes of snow
hiss lightly on the glazes
and gather into drops
that the empty air will inhale.

We carry our unfired flesh
through atmospheres and climates
that wait for our decay,
expecting things alive
to take on the life of things.
Change drifts down on our heads
from a past mediated
by mason, shaman, priest—
all those who learned the secret
that the seed must be buried to live,
caught up in atmospheres,
loosening into vapor,
tightening into snowflake.

IL SE SAUVE

*"He saw that he had lost his fear of falling
and all other fears of that nature."*   JOHN CHEEVER

More like a well than a dungeon,
more like a cave than a jail,
the cell shows shadow figures on its wall.
Can such semblances of truth keep
men captive closer
than whip-wielding mistresses
and swag-belted sheriffs? The convicted
tumble into their own preparations—
punjjis, nooses, petards.
Every teaspoon of punishment has been anticipated.

Saints and prisoners embrace such exercises as
pushups, double-entry computations,
mnemonics, and other apportionments.
They write about pilgrims, knights-errant,
victims of illusion. All they need
to expose the vast illusion of prisons
is the wings of an angel.

Even a peregrine's flight may be bribed.
A falconer deceives his hawk with a hood
to which she surrenders in an orderly sequence
of decisions, becoming accustomed
to jesses, gantlets, darkness,
gobbets of dead meat,
rations of light and flight.
The falcon, no angel,
chooses to submit.

The cell itself becomes the enemy.
To accept the minimum security of life,
wings must fall from the shoulders.
Among shadows and sentences you remember
when you could have made a break for it,
when, if you had had the wings of an angel,
you could have got out of here,
uplifted, saved yourself.

THE SWORDLESS STATUE

(Thomas Ball's "Washington," Boston Public Garden)

A starling sits on the general's hat.
   No sword adorns the empty hand,
yet Washington glares at our hotel
   without surrendering command.

Sculptors and metallists many times
   have filled his hand with substitute steel
to animate the great parade.
   We sit at the Ritz, toy with a meal,

and contemplate how lights illume
   the verdigris Virginian's force,
his garnished grip. Yet knees and thighs
   and reins will hardly urge a horse

if stallion nostrils snort no steam,
   if balls hang green and bare,
if any child can steal a sword
   from the general, riding there.

TWO MIDRASHIM

1. *Untuned String* (PSALM 90)

> *"Yea, the work of our hands, establish thou it."*

My childhood Steinway spoke in tongues
(*Liebesleid, lacrimae rerum, ostinato*)
when other people played it.
Sometimes a visitor—Lhevinne, Sykes, Raieff—
could make the family instrument talk turkey,
but when I perched up tight between its legs
my stubby fingers whacked out sounds
that broke the bright charge of music.

O god in the machine! You have cast
a penumbra of sound across all memory,
the purple garment of Europe I wear,
my American secret. And you strike
an even darker note: something's amiss with my hands.
I can carry a tune only with voices.
Never fit to manage
the nineteenth century's noblest invention,
(the one that enabled mere men
to establish the work of their hands)
I am shut out from taking a hand in sonatas,
dismissed from polonaise, mazurka, prelude, fugue,
mordant, glissando, thoroughbass.
I may not harrow music with my hands.
I'm struck dumb by a pentecost of piano.

2. *Darkheart* (JOB 19:26)

The scientist of the night
and the walker in the city
convey me, one at each elbow,
over the shadows of anger
toward my unwillingness.
Wakeful and stiff,
I glower in the darkness
with eyes that will not aid
my body to seek the light.

How graceless to deny
that grunt of understanding:
that only *in my flesh*
shall I see God!

THE LAUGHTER OF WOMEN

When men go out for laughs, they give their all,
baring their teeth, betraying no memory
of the slave quarters, master's rumpled bed,
heaps of hacked corpses at the river crossing,
bodies bent back in alleyways or gardens.
Men's voices rise and sharpen nasally
to slice even their brothers off at the knees,
ho-hoing at the gallons of booze, the babes
the other put away the night before.
"Hey Roy, better shut your eyes
before you bleed to death."

The laughter of women holds a world at bay,
whether through giggles of girls leering askance
at the hulking narcissistic strut of an athlete,
or with the hushed laughter of a fiancée
feeling a stranger's eyes stroking her breasts,
or in the stylized *ha-ha* of zarzuela dancers
(hand on one hip, flower in the teeth,
wrist flung overhead like a whiplash).
Laughter gives women strength, protection, help,
making men wonder what their secret is.

"We know your ways," men hear that laughter say.
"As girls we bathed and dressed boy babies
and cannot disremember what you are.
Though swaying to your sex, should we not fear
that love will promptly turn away its face
the day we trust you to implant a life?
To make light of man's yoke, that costly burden,
we laugh at the dark, the dark that pulls us down."
The laughter of a woman is her pride.
Men smile and shake their heads to think of it,
how gladly women wear their rings, their houses.
The heads of women lean together, laughing.

SLEEPING BEAUTY VARIATIONS

(for Peter Shaffer)

Marriage or poison. Which was the gift
   that struck princes limp at the castle wall
like stones become too heavy to lift?

Matchmaker smirked, courtiers sniffed,
   godmother grinned from the head of the hall.
Marriage or poison, which was the gift?

Supple Aurora, maiden adrift,
   sheds blood, turns woman and takes the fall,
stone become too heavy to lift.

The world knows ways to give short shrift
   to sex that smothers itself in a pall
of marriage or poison. Which *was* the gift?

Upstairs the sleepers stir and shift.
   Time trickles down to bury us all,
stones become too heavy to lift.

The race we know is not to the swift.
   Slow sleeps out his life in a stall.
   Marriage or poison, which was the gift?
The stone become too heavy to lift?

JANUARY 1977

You had "never been absent." The nation hissed
   with blizzards. Telephone rang:
your voice from Tulsa. My heart and tongue
   interfered to say no more than
      "I miss you,"

blotting out news of white skies that had frozen
   sheep dead where they stood,
news of the illness of children. My love
   for your body skated across
a continent chilled to its heart with low temperatures
     setting new records.

Your voice had faded. Dreams reinforced
   the remoteness: I'm shut from our house,
from your bed, kneeling bareshins in slush.
   Dream islands breed
poisoned shellfish, dream bridges
   won't reach. My hands
tingled to cup your breast but shut
     as cold as the plains.

NEW YEAR'S EVE

The club is filling, tables draped with linen.
Behind the scenes waiters open wine.
Early arrivals are already tabled in corners.
I scurry to a bathroom to cover up, for
a ceremony is in the making. I cannot qualify
until I'm dressed in stiff shirt, shiny shoes,
black tie wrestled by trembling fingers,
jacket with shiny lapels.
The more I dress, the more I'm like the others;
the more I dress, the more invisible;
the more I dress, the more alone.

Now, seated at the rout, right hand around a glass
of clearest gin, I nod and smile at the penguins.
Soon—another sip of gin—
the door will swing wide and admit, from the outside dark,
spectres of the women I have loved.
Here's the head of one, the breasts of another, the silky
hair of a third, the perfume of a fourth,
the wetness of another long forgotten.

I stand and watch the broad one, the tall one, the small one.
Before my eyes they merge into one woman.
I'd have one girl take all the flaming decades
and burn them to cinders with her clear blue eyes.

ON ITHACA

Settling at home, after Calypso, Circe
and Nausicaa, in Penelope's olive-tree bed,
among flocks of sheep and swine, surrounded by orchards,
how will Odysseus die? Will Penelope fuck him to death?
Or will he take to drinking with the swineherds?
In a pool Odysseus regards his body, comely
as when the women bathed it, and Athene
touched it with ambrosia till it glowed.
Later, abed, he dreams of Polyphemus,
the red-hot stake, the shriek, the sizzling eyeball,
that other flock of sheep, the great ram for escape,
the suitors feasting in the high-roofed hall,
the gouts of blood that spurted from his arrows.

WORDLESS WINTER

1. *Clinical Depression*

who cares what name you call it   here it comes
curling around the house in the dark like mist
that has no dampness   settling on my chest
like a weightless bird   tell it to go away
shout   clap your hands   let them stare
this visitor has no parents   where it lives
when it isnt invading innocent islands
I cannot guess for the life of me   I guess
it must have habitation in my cells
imprisoned like a foaming lunatic   shaking
the bars of my body   keeping the entire penitentiary
awake   baying me moonward night after night

who has seen low pressure   neither you nor I
but to deny the fact of my possession by it
is to declare myself swept clean of devils
and weep   goodbye depression   hello anxiety

2. *The Clinic*

When you say, "You haven't
done anything wrong," you must mean
that if I had done it, it could not be wrong,
being my act.

Such high regard the doctor
professes for the patient! That my most
ravenous desire should be characterized
as innocently as a pail of milk,
or one leg thrown dreamily over another!

Could you have meant that all sins
are equal, that there's "nothing
abnormal" in such behavior?

Then fact steps up with more
than moral news: *We found
cancer cells on the slide.*

You declare, "You haven't done
anything wrong." And I reply,
    "Haven't I?"

3.   *Willing Her to Live*

O, she's dying all right. But maybe
no faster than anyone else,
as Mark Twain said in response
to certain inquiries.
Among the remnants of a harvest,
sweating and staring in my garden,
I shovel dark infusions of manure
across pale autumn soil
in layers of enriching history,
stuff that cattle had devoured,
chewed over, passed through
before keeping a date with the butcher.

As I excite topsoil for next year
I wonder who will eat what's not yet grown
or whether anyone will plant it.
Wetly, blindly I keep shovelling.
Earth snatches compost back
like a transfusion and will not pause
to keep a leaf attached
in response to prayers or tears
or the use of shovels.

4.   *Frozen Drought*

Surprising sunshine has ruled more than a hundred days
this bare winter. Snow has forgotten itself.
The ground lies hard as stone and flat with dust

as though the surface were peeling in the wind
and blowing off to hell or to dust-heaven.
Neighbors and newspapers speak of the oddity,
snowless New England! Week after week blows by
and the ground grows dryer and the teeth grit.
The nose seals up against an invasion
of drought in Eastern air that never tasted
the brown dark of the dust over bleeding Kansas.

5. *Householder*

What can explain this ebb-tide of emotion,
this failure of joints and parts,
this position, as intolerable as
a turned turtle?
Hand will not clench on its pen,
head mislays its calling.
Heart? Content to keep beating.

This unfever has its blessings:
the bleaching out of anger.
A sensibility confined
to the predictable.
Indoor plants, domesticated animals.
No wild birds, no wild weather.
An implacable appetite
for things as they are. A nice gratitude
for the unresisted passage of time.

As householder I have felt
entitled to hope for better.
Now I pray to keep out of bed,
ask for no worse.
My friends hear nothing from me
once highly regarded, nor
do my enemies.
I have been taught by mixed blessings,
poisoned apples,
to sit apart, muscles clenched like marble.

6. *Stalemate*

Her will has worked
to the surface,
outcarving that smooth
genetic chisel that incised
rills running like inlets
toward her cornflower-blue eyes.
I kiss their corners.

Whatever it is that keeps
her harnessed
to the burden of her body
has impressed a set
of stretch marks on the forehead—
reinforcements.

Her face, a landscape, carries
the colors of contending armies:
a tug of joy, eyes lit with laughter;
a nagging hermit mask;
a cloud of pain.

7. *After Winter Slaughtering*

Our pigs have spent weeks away from their pen,
but hoofprints frozen in midnight mud
remember in ice the shape of a thigh
that, slaughtered, severed, relieved of blood,
lies cold in the dark as a blinded eye
counting lineup shots of arrested men.

8. *The Writing Lesson*

Miss Daisy M. Johnston enforced her rules:
no wiggling, talking, or gum.
Hands clasped, or flat on the desk,
never out of sight in the lap.
Miss Daisy gospelled the Palmer Method:
write, write, write with the arm, not with the fingers;
push and pull as though conducting music.
The pencil must be held airily, unsqueezed,
guided through wrist, thumb, and elbow,
mastered by the shoulder,
guided by the waist.

Who, learning letters in this fashion,
could reserve adequate breath
to shriek for help
when muscles clenched in complaint
and the center of the body disclaimed them
and the poet, hands flat on the desk,
no wiggling, talking, or gum,
felt the dark cadence castigate his arm?

MY LADY THE LAKE

It is the lake within the lake that drowns.
Sunbeams gnaw into its dark, never again
to be released as light. The lake swallows
whatever it is fed. It eats its ice each spring,
nibbles for years at fallen twigs and timber,
engorges the heat of summer with each sunset,
closes around corpse of dragonfly and beaver.
By its waters I have sat down and wept, without
taking any comfort or return
except for the offer of what it has translated:
frogs, crayfish, sticklebacks. The trout
stocked by a prescient owner crammed themselves,
after the passage of several seasons, up
against its banks to die. It devoured their bones.
Still water gives us only a reflection.
Whatever we cast in, it will accept,
and in such lakes within the lake we drown.

PRAYING WRONG

(*1984*)

To the memory of Jane Truslow Davison
and for our children, Angus and Lesley

WINTERING OVER

Only spring sun, so tense, so pale,
so unestablished, could manage the matter,
but once again as every year
this weathered old beast
unfolds a plan to hurl
a filament of itself
across the arroyo
and build its annual bridge
between past and future.
If I stand back, keep
an eye on things, I may
witness my own delivery
from high above the female proscenium,
cave of fertility and its enactment.
This event is me. Do I know it?
Am I this very thing?
I answer my own questions.
An intimate galaxy of genes
reiterates the permanence of change,
and this great attic of language,
lovingly rummaged,
will welcome a fresh brood of tenants
into the most tumbledown of houses.

Let us live here.

THE VANISHING POINT

(New Year's Day 1984)

Snow crept up overnight as we slept
and powdered the surface of the earth so lightly
the footpaths stirred, as smooth as dusted skin.
An uncut beard of grass darkened the field.
I had awakened to the shimmering landscape
from a sleep sunk in sullen dreams, entombed
in the companionship of friends long dead
who accelerated along gravel country roads
or city streets crammed with traffic
toward no end anyone would have wanted to reach.
Their destination was a point deeper than ever
in the closed and unforgiving past
where love enacts its remorseless guzzling.

This morning, though, was dusted with the present
as though brushed by the smoky fragrance
of sleep. It held there for the moment.
No wind stirred up the snow along the branches,
no wheel crushed down a snowflake on the road.
This present moment, exquisitely poised,
had not yet given in to the scramble of time
but seemed to hold itself back from moving on
out of a night which hurtled in drunken zigzags
through one of the dreams where we are never alone.
Carried by trains, motorcycles, elevators,
we are always passengers, always companioned,
sniffing out the smelly trails of childhood,
flaunting a thousand newly-sewn disguises.
Where those dreams take us, no matter how eager
their search, they never end in arrival.

Now the present is inching toward the future.
At the silent feeding station chickadees chirp.
Over the marsh black air flourishes flecks
of irregular white, more snowflakes, *storme still.*
The sky as it unbends relents a little
and grows lighter. A dog barks in protest

at the iron day, indignant at its silence.
The perfection of this morning hour has yielded,
without anticipation, to the fact
that time is coasting forward, turning momentum
into the new year's elliptical glide.

Poised on the incoming day, between tides
of sleep and waking, I ride on the waters of time,
whose movement, steady as the orb of earth,
makes only one general statement: *Change is all.*
The weather system, the troubling dreams of travel,
a scrap of geography discarded here
in the glacial scree of leftover landscape—
these happenings seek no end, no destination.
Each moment wishes us to move farther on
into a sequence we can follow at most
to vanishing point. We can see no farther,
though time seems to pause and wait for us at times
and measure us and move along again.

THE HOUSEWIFE'S PARADISE

Across the scene dance dromedaries,
tigers, prancing horses, zebras,
"two and two of all flesh
wherein is the breath of life."
The sceptre tail of Lion commands
a procession of beasts under father trees.
The sky has clouded over. Waters gurgle
to tug the ark by its hull. Will Noah preserve
one pair of every sort of genital,
the periphrastic families of the earth?

In Pennsylvania preacher Edward Hicks,
fleeing from ghostly swords,
peered through the branches of a half-cut forest
and brushed in scenes of peaceful time-to-come
as promised in plain statements by the Lord.
A hatted Quaker smacked a friendly palm
against a feathered red man's on a beach.
Smiling Lion crouched to nibble hay
by the side of pussycat Ox.
Leaves did not tumble, wounds did not leak blood,
lambkins never crumpled in a colic.
Rooftops, safe against God's lightning,
kept rainspots off the pewter plates of housewives,
sheltering the honeyed entropies of peace.

On working farms the gravid ewes give
bloody birth on bare barn floors. The lambs
lie there, at first unblinking. Mothers lick
mucus from the nostrils and the eyes,
and offspring totter to suck at the flesh
that further heats their breath.
In May longlight, February lambs
may drop the teat and munch the sea of grass
as noisily as their great toothed sisters,
and then, why not, next fall, be mounted
by the greedy-shouldered ram
with gasps of satisfaction, breath of life?

In Hicks' landscapes horses won't gallop:
they prance, curvet, lie at rest.
Even George Washington's steed stands easy,
deaf to captains and the shouting.
The Peaceable Kingdom, shelter for Friends,
shelters them coolly under a cloudless roof
in a clearing as solid as a square stone house.

Here is the land of cider, laundry, bread,
the housewife's paradise, with love lavishly spread
in quilt or bright-scrubbed doorstep
to shed its inner light
and banish every howling of the spirit.
Cast it out elsewhere, anywhere you will,
and pit the blessed order of a kitchen shelf
against the barbarism of the kill.

QUESTIONS OF SWIMMING, 1935

(For Robert Penn Warren)

What was the nub of wonder? Was it
the man, giant to my child-eyes, strapping
a shiny black rubber bathing cap over the cap
of his red hair, plugging his nostrils and ears,
and lowering his lean body into the yellow
lake in Colorado, down into the frightening
water, to begin the steady trudgen
that took him, as long as my skipping patience
could endure, steadily farther from sight
as far as the far shore, a mile, and without
pause, brought him back to me, bobbing
far out in the water, then thrashing,
then finally splashing, and gasping and rising,
and then, again, human and near me, dripping and walking?

Wonder at the man, or at the task?
What sort of way was it to spend
an hour in thrashing straight across a lake
and, turning, swimming straight back to the start?
Where was he setting out for when he began, fresh?
Where had he been to when he returned, winded?

Or take the style: laboring akimbo,
a steady crawl across the sheet of water
without a pause to whoop or whistle or blow,
a style as awkward as inexorable,
in which the completion of the task seemed to count
more to the swimmer than not drowning.

The lake? A captive body
the dry climate had permitted
to rest between the knees
Boulder had bulldozed to keep

the water from evaporating: a reservoir.
The man swam back and forth between its walls.

What of the rhythm of the exercise?
Not like a dog or deer that simply walks
on water, but a dactyl, a quantitative
excursus, a distribution of forces between
the limbs, these legs working like scissors,
these arms working like flails, these lungs
working like bellows, this mind working,
working on lessened oxygen, this body
moving against every interference to imitate
its forgotten grandfather, the fish.

To the destructive element submit yourself,
and with the exertions of your hands and feet
make the deep, deep sea keep you up.
Once kept up, where do we go from there?
To the headwaters, the spawning ground?
To the floating pyre, the fire ship?
To the other shore? Which is the other shore?
Could it be the place where a boy could watch
a man pull on the helmet of a bathing cap
and set out, swimming, for a farther shore?

LOW LANDS

(For Jacob van Ruysdael and for John Updike)

This topsoil coverlet, dampened by a coast
that's warmed by mediation of the sea,
shall be transformed—I'll paint them!—into hills
erected by a netherlander's fancy,
crags bearing castles and churches, theologies
for which a million suffering soldiers died.

A birch tree, blasted, leans along one border
to balance the other, a dark insolent rainbow.
Between the two a castle falls to ruin.
Light burns inside the trunks of standing trees,
gleams in the rump of a carthorse going to water.
See how this goat hesitates, beside a ford,
whether to cross over to the side of the angels?
"Hunting a Stag": the doomed innocent quarry
plashes ill-suited hooves across a marsh,
unsparingly pursued by dogs, hunters,
and the light and shade from several hundred trees.
Above this scene hawks, vultures, owls and doves
read speeches from the drama of salvation.

I will distend the hummock's trickling water
by doubling the distance it can fall.
Infirm foundations lift my tottering spires.
Hills that my parish eyes have elevated
will bulge up higher, skyward, birdward, Godward,
belittling the cities of the plain,
the fishing fleets, plowed fields, hedged pastures
whose view gives no more length than the horizon.
From Italy I shall import a landscape
that some of us prefer to thoughts of heaven,
transforming lowlands into the lofty hills
which the Most High desired for His abode.

INTIMACIES

1. *Mates*

Stronger than vows or roses is the scent
that gathers from a sweet conjunction of lives,
as when two animals, nosing into love,
have snouted each other's parts and found them good.
Each such discovery discovers more,
roaming savannah, sousing in mire, snoring in caves.
When the mood strikes they strike out in different directions,
expecting to slouch to some waterhole at sunset
where, after dark, they will curl up together,
nose to tail, as easy as potatoes.

2. *Prints*

Hoofprints of a plowhorse!
who's trampled steelshod
from end to end of the flower bed,
filing in front of one stalk
of withered delphinium
but threading behind another
along the granite wall.
There the prints vanished.
Oh, how I glowered
at such brutal trespass!
And when I walked out
to steal a second look
even worse had taken place:
a filigree of fox tracks
printed primly inside
the massive dents of hoof,
passing by the wall,
sparing the flowers.

ABSALOM

King David's anguish bristled,
whimpered, cocked his head
like a lost hound
listening for its master.
The prince crazed into a muddle
of tears at every teaching.
Riddles sent him areel.

What of such a son, whose father
refuses to do him harm
but turns away his face?
Could he ever earn the right
to inherit the crown of Saul
until he felt emboldened,
like his father before him,
to put on the unthinkable colors
of the king's worst enemy?

This too sent him areel.
Why not, he must have thought,
get dressed in overalls
and gallop off on a mule
along the first track to the left?
This led him, as it happened,
in under a stunted
ruin of an oak,

and now he hangs there, helpless,
target for the average man,
doomed by the tendrils
of human hair
he couldn't help growing,

and the king, as helpless as he
in the chamber above the gate,
covers his face again:
Would God I had died for thee,
O Absalom, my son, my son!

CROSSING THE VOID

(for Stanley Kunitz)

I pick my crooked way
across a half-built bridge
past left-behind lunchpails,
rusting wrenches, cables
coiled scattershot
half across the span.
Could my scream be heard?
No, nor anyone catch
a glimpse of a body falling
to the rocks, hammered to pieces
by the brawling stream below.

I count my footsteps toward
the emptiness ahead
with no memory pushing me,
not the milk-scented kisses of childhood,
nor the prickle of revenge,
nor the black hounds of grief.
Against my face
droplets of flannel mist
dash tiny explosions.

Misguided by travel,
I know that without ground
I can hear no music, yet
unless I go on I'll be barred
from footing ashore
in rigging, on bridges,
clambering or crossing. As I approach
the vanishing point, I begin to feel
a half-remembered sickness
as when the waterfilled seaboot
pulls down, and then the list,
heave and plunge
of sinking planking.

THE MONEY CRY

My daughter cries when we have to talk about money.
"I can't help it," she wails. "I don't want to cry,
I just cry." How can a father blame her?
I set her straight by setting her allowance
or trying to mold the world to snug her budget
or preaching homilies about expense
and self-sufficiency. Foresight. *Foresight.*
All the while, quietly, helplessly, she cries.

Dollars of course can give a girl her head
with beads and shawls, or buy her sweet shampoos
and the acrid clangor of recorded music.
But dollars too could set her hands to work,
scrubbing pots and pans, mucking out stables.
No wonder money makes her cry! I can't
help wincing when I sit to pay the bills
from Progressive Oil or Dr. Leon Leach,
recalling the time it cost to raise the money.
I shiver when paychecks hiss across my blotter.
What will smear off? What is the handling charge?

I'd warn you to be wary of anyone
whose eyes light up at each percentage point
as though life were an electronic game
with nothing to describe it but the score.
The hunt's the game, not the computation,
yet all the while the world presents its bills,
and we sit paying them on Friday night
while everybody else is at the movies.
Listen! Don't cry. You get it and you spend it.
Take it and pass it on. That stuff won't kill you.

LAST INFIRMITY

O poem, poem! What possibility
has either of us got to be remembered
unless we can appeal over my head?
What if next Tuesday as I cross the street
that takes me to the cleaners I should walk
under the wheels of a truck (Calvucci & Sons/
Produce/ Revere Mass) while thinking of
a way to the right result in Nicaragua?
What would become of dear unfinished you,
crammed dogeared in a folder, vulnerable phrases
half-scratched-out? Whose hand then would smooth you,
uncrumple you, berate you? You and I
would have to take a powder together, ashes
in a tarnished urn, scraps of desperate paper
scuttling across the dump, your message whelmed
by the flurry of a thousand scavenger gulls.

NOTHING SUDDEN

1. *Monosyllables*

Here, says hot body,
stretched under pines
tossed by a westerly,
here, says skin.

Now, say sharp senses,
dizzied by mockingbirds
in the wisteria,
now, say ears.

This, say fingerpads,
dabbling along a plank
where the grain roughens,
this, says touch.

Wait, says the quick breath
at the first quiver
of a thigh stirring,
wait, says love.

See, says inquisitor,
flaying the pagan
ribcage from backbone,
that says *kill*.

I, says abandonment,
whispering hot words
to a cold pillow,
I, says husk.

Then? says memory,
then I was just a child,
then I loved tenderly.
Then, says echo.

Down, says the petal-fall.
Down, says the prophet.
Down down derry down
down, says drastic.

2.   *Night Watch*

Behind the sooty hill a violet sky
turns purple as the earth vanishes.
House-finches, nuthatches drop their suet
to wing for the woods.
The last of the daytime gulls has flapped away
to outer, colder islands.
In the who-hours an owl, downpasture,
breathes its wicked song from the pear-tree.

Tomorrow, many wakeful hours away,
when the sun singles out the feeding station,
faded goldfinch, chickadee, grosbeak and titmouse
will already have come from the woods.
The night-warmed dog will be whimpering
once again for the truth of open air.
Gravid sheep, restless, cramped
after their huge night in the black barn,
will be crowding the gate of their pen,
edging one another aside
to make a break when the gate swings.

What else is there to expect?
Things, beasts, want out, want in.
Behind those curtains can she still be sleeping?

3. *Moving into Memory*

As long as those last words are never spoken
we can touch each other lightly
and sit here side by side
in the descending sun.
Our hands often creep
into one another's palms:
every other form of seeking
has gone lame or dry.
O dark sunbeam, my bed light, my cheer,
brightener of houses, freshener of shade,
the only gift I can be sure to keep
is this reaching and touching.
You will be allowed to keep nothing.

I keep unsure memory, and none.
The piano, glittering under delectable mountains,
has lost its way to the center of the music.
Silence gapes to swallow
the provocations of your laughter.
Though our days together are few,
the thunder of syllables
fills a black valley with light
while the wind whistles its own song
from the faraway edge of the glacier.

4. *Stern Stuff*

The ashes, done up in stiff white paper
with hospital folds sealed over at each end,
lie dizzily beside the hole we've dug.
Tan talcum silt, powdered by two years' drought,
sifts out of a shovel. We watch the canister
tumble into the hole and lie alone.
Those ashes, while they held their lively form,
glowed flowery with every kind of laughter
and drove an ingenuity of will
to keep her vivid in a fading world.

Is this how we choke, in cataracts of dust?
What stern stuff it is, crumpling
the twigs of brittle, lace-veined wings
and chafing the light from smoky diamond eyes.

5.   *Remembering Eurydice*

I have lost the best of women.
Once again water irrigates
the scars, the gravel.
It was nothing sudden:
death set a stamp on her body
but not on her laughter.
We cowered together like children
at a flash of lightning,
imagining whether it would strike,
learning the tune of truth.

In a meadow peppered with daisies
she hung a screened tent
where she could be shaded
to tell the hours of summer,
gazing across pastures
where sheep grazed, paused
to wonder at the woman
seated, sorrowing.
Only her dog, mutely
privy to her loss of stance,
watched her tidy up her life's house
alone. When friends came
she smiled to keep them from grieving.

Now we can barely remember,
while woods and grasses
which remember nothing
offer us all we have to keep
but the stone that cries her name.

6. *The Everlasting*

A fist of flowers, anonymous as prayers,
a dozen field-plucked purple asters, droop
prone on a ledge a yard below that name
chased deep into harsh rock. Only four letters,
forty-nine years dismembered by a dash, peep pink
from the thorax of the granite ledge she loved.
Some florist roses fill a water glass
leaning atilt beneath the ledge's foot.
I can guess at the names of those who gathered flowers
or forked a couple of bills across a counter,
but, as the petals wilt below a name
that will outlast all eyes that read it now,
they speak as well as names or voices can
about fragility, flowering, fading away:
they speak for frost and death. The asters speak
out of a world of change, of repetition,
for those events that only happen once.

7. *The Revenant*

Last night, rummaging for scissors
in a back drawer, his fingers touched
something alive, not alive,
a pouch concealed under papers,
an envelope with no address.
In it, a lock of graying hair,
lopped from her head before the Cytoxin, cure-all,
not able to save her,
had struck her bald.
His hand now cradled one part
that had sprouted from her body,
many times assenting to
the touch of his fingers.
Her hair! The only frailty
she'd admit to! Her doctor,
never lowering his gaze,
told her she had a year to go,

adding of course he could "make her
more comfortable" with chemotherapy.
Her hands flew to her head, frightened birds
to save her hair. They fell at once
fluttering to her lap. She had to laugh
at herself, the hands. But not at the hair.
"I'm sorry," she said, aghast
at her own reasons.

THE GREAT LEDGE

(*1989*)

FOR JOAN

EQUINOX 1980

In the stillness after dawn we two
     paddled a noiseless boat
before wakefall across
     a bay smooth as a mirror,
changeless as its glass.
     Not a whisper of passage.
Hardly a single stir
     inside the horizon
except for the rippling
     wrinkles pushed by our prow
and the faraway swoop and flurry
     of a squadron of terns.
The tide at its landward edge
     ignited a smudge of commotion,
skittering sandpipers
     along the farther shore.
In all the days of our marriage
     we had never seen
so unruffled a morning:
     never had any event
shimmered with so costly a light
     as we ascended the meandering
creek in our sweet boat,
     surprising no one except
a bright-eyed otter.
     Pushed by mere hints
from our paddles,
     we rode up the thickening tide
among heavy wands
     of ripe marsh grass
that wagged seed-bundles
     high above our heads.

Neither one speaking,
     we rose to go ashore
and lugged away
     our featherweight kayak
to winter quarters,

     knowing as we stowed it
that this would be the last time,
     that we would never set out to sea
together again.

SECOND NESTING

(for J. E. G.)

Oh, you and I have feathered our new nest
with webs of straw and string, what we've collected
in earlier migrations, things beaked up at random
by roadside, woodland, pebbles or manmade shards
that winked and caught the eye of one or the other.

Let's call this springtime—springtime in late summer.
Now that the chicks have fattened, feathered and flown,
let's start over again. We hope we've learned
from earlier nestings knowledge of comfort and joy,
ways of diffusing danger before it arrives.

Mold every room into the shapes of shelter,
a shaft of sun, made captive in mid-city;
chimneys of reassurance by the marsh;
the wooden lovenest nestling in the woods.

Each of these perches gives us nourishment—
we two who, city-born, have taken Place
and made a worship of it—two who breathe ourselves
through landscape, carry secrets that we hug
close to the heart, the body's aquifer,
certain that every flight will bring us home.

UNSUNG HOURS

Out in the dark, rain
spatters the leather
of late-summer beech leaves
while we, no more than half awake,
barely moving, hardly in touch,
lie closer together
than if we sagged grossly asleep
or tensed into arousal.
The back of one leg rests
against the front of the other.
Arms tangle together. Who
can remember, or care, which
body each belongs to,
as long as, half waking, we float
through sleep as in a canoe?
This time of night holds
more intimacy than passion.
Beyond gifts, caresses or quarrels
these unspoken passages, these
unsung hours excite the inklings
of poets, thicken the palette
the painter scrapes
to entice his equilibrium
of color, stir what the musician
carries in sweet cadences
of closing. To save these unsung
states of possession,
we'd have to fall away
toward the unremembered depths of sleep.

THE FACE IN THE FIELD

The meadow yielded thirteen bales an acre.
"Was that a record?" I asked one of the experts.
"It must have been a record. When was the last time
you manured that meadow? Eighteen eighty-one?"
Yet it is beautiful, whether mowed or not.
After its saddest harvest, stubble bristled
sparsely, yet the stalks stood up like Christians.
Now that the second crop is coming in,
it bends to the wind as if a hand had stroked it.
Here there's a patch of purple-colored fescue
that glistens metallic at the heart of summer;
there, dogbane creeps in on the heels of the mowing
to hold its tiny white blossoms as a girl does,
stooping to drink, clutching beads to her breast
to keep them from getting wet in the fountain.

High to the south where maps mark The Great Ledge
is where my father's ashes tumbled down.
Ten years after them, his widow's followed.
Low to the north, gazing up at the Ledge,
another outcrop from the field, a ledge
of pink-and-green-flecked granite, with a pinch
of silver sprinkled over its harsh surface,
speaks the word JANE for her who has become
familiar of the place, but was once its mistress.

How difficult to keep her face in mind
as part of a living body! The body lives on,
sometimes remembered in my arms and fingers,
but the face that spoke to me with eyes and throat
resists replacement. Yet it will live on,
a vagueness in the grass, a ghost among trees.
I have stared out a thousand times across
the field, hoping to see what she
rested her eyes upon while she was dying,
but I can see nothing there beyond the leaves.
They were happy enough to speak to me before,
whatever it is that leaves and trees will speak of,

but how can they now so wholly have possessed
the country that she took the time to die in?
Perhaps it's just as well. Remembered things
should not survive by long the death of the body.
See? Every year the grass renews itself
with shoots and leaves and, ultimately, flowers.

THE FARM ANIMALS' DESERTION

Where have you gone, O cherished Lexington,
tiptoe red-spotted pig? Or you, proud Hoppy,
brandishing your pair of spiralled horns
martial as General Joshua? You, poor Chipmunk?
Holding to life inside your mother's womb
till the police force lent their Smith & Wesson
to let you out of your mother? We cut you free.
Soon you were bawling for seven bottles a day
and looming over your cousins. How many lambs
did you give us to graze before you were "retired"?
(Breed them a year too long, and you can split
those old ewes right in half.)
                              Chipmunk's gone
like Hoppy and Lexington, Concord, Nick and Chops.
The pasture's eerily empty, cropped and trampled
with a thousand cuneiform marks. Fenceposts sag
under the weight of the half-mile of wire
we hung to keep dogs from getting at the sheep
and to keep sheep from getting at the roses.
Nothing but birdcalls fill the pasture now,
no grunt from pigpen, no baa from under the barn,
no clop of goat's soft hooves upon the rock.

Here, isolated in the house, we childless bipeds,
no longer fit to breed or put to stud,
consume more stuff than we can ever produce,
filling up shelter that could shelter others.
Our ladder's rickety, the one that led
up to the hayloft, to the vanished world
we fertilized in fields that now lie fallow
like all the million acres of New England
that bear no crop except these rags, these bones.

OPENING UP

Weekend: a country custom, a century old,
English in origin, secular, elite,
depended on railway schedules for its ritual:
breakfast in silver warmers, tweeds till tea,
tennis or crocquet when there was no hunting,
dress for dinner, billiards after port,
later, adultery in upstairs bedrooms.

Now as the car turns willingly off asphalt
and gravel stings its tires, we try our hand.
Arriving's all the same, though all has changed.
The buds have swollen; or the leaves have turned;
the house is still surprisingly intact.
An unlocked door will let the world back in—
groceries, canvas satchels, lists of chores.

Stop. Watch the maples bending in the wind
tossing their boughs in summer agitation.
Quick, before sunset, swim the salt creek
that creeps up from the coast a mile away
to hiss beneath the bridges, trickle through
the swaying stalks of marsh grass, burdened with
more nourishment than twenty tons of humus.
Here one is happiest when not too clean.

Come on, walk barefoot over new-cut stalks
of green lawn grass, pausing to wipe off
the sticky blades that squeeze between your toes.
Along the granite of the garden wall
a hundred varied blossoms flash their hues
of gold and scarlet, peach and ivory.

One skyscraper stands up among the lilies,
brandishing blossoms like archangels' trumpets—
all while the thirsty grasses dream the day.
Bend toward them. I can hear the tide of green
engorge and stiffen, music in the blood,
lifting sensation past the reach of time,
mingling with the future. Come, let's turn,
let's walk indoors and open up the house.

THE GREAT LEDGE

The fox, as she picked her path along the wall,
caught sight of me, stopped, pricked her ears up, loped,
no hint of hurry, over a swatch of wetland
and vanished at the foot of the Great Ledge.
To track her I'd have to climb a cliff
whose top is riddled with the mouths of lairs:
rabbits and chipmunks burrow the simple soil,
raccoons carve lodges underneath the roofs
of overhanging ledges. Woodchucks gouge
dens at the edges of embedded stone.
Deer, in the swamp below, nibble at maple buds
in winter, shelter in the thick entanglements
that later on will send displays of scarlet
fluttering over the swamp at summer's end,
and light a fire of marigolds next spring.

Nearly a hundred vertical feet of granite
hem in the faltering stream that trickles by.
It sets a barrier scarp for the frozen brine
that under winter pressure tilts on edge
and clicks against the Ledge's foot. Then, melting,
it mixes the sweet brook with salty sea,
the finite with the almost infinite.
Just at this boundary of sea and land
a ruined rowboat rots, half overgrown
by waterweeds, a longtime telltale
for what belongs to ocean, what to woods.
In spring the ibis comes to perch upon it:
here from the woodlot we can watch the ibis feed.

High as a judge, its shoulders robed with pine,
its granite facing north and faintly tinged
with grey-green lichen, towers the Great Ledge.
It takes a titled place on every map
that locals or surveyors have sketched out
the last three hundred years, and before that
it served as landmark for Conomo Indians
in journeys from their winter hunting grounds
to summertime seaside encampments, where
they'd loll and roast their bluefish. They have left
great heaps of shattered clamshells by the shore,
just as they buried their bones atop the hills
to rest at length within sound of the sea.
Such hilltop graves, larded with human dead,
pointed new trespassers in misdirections.

Three centuries ago one fisherman
planted a farmhouse hard by the creekside,
close to the seeming shelter of the Ledge—
too close, perhaps, for comfort. In the 1860's
his sly successor started once again
and built, square to the sun, a house so poised
it let each breath of summer cool his cheek
yet split the force of northeast storms, so that
the wind would leave his drive swept bare, clean—
six feet of snowbank layered behind the house
and an escape route whiskbroomed to the road.
He set his cow-barn high, to mediate
between the human comforts of the house
and the harsh granite of reality:
he'd need not walk a rod toward the east
or west before the Ledge loomed up, year-round,
to set its imprint on his acreage,
whether for lazing livestock, or the woodland beasts
that sheltered in its lee, or for the men
who learned to look away and hurry on
without requiring explanations.

The Great Ledge looked on as the glacier failed
and left each hilltop scoured by retreat,
its melting trickling in to heal its wound.
The creek welled up and blanketed the rubble
with silt and muck: mattresses for seed
of plants that the vigor of the tide might rinse
and fertilize. Shortly a billion minnows
nibbled and panicked under a summer sun,
banquets for predators. Millions would escape
to populate the undiscouraged sea
by surging on spring tides to sprinkle eggs
in the tepid murk of the surrounding shallows
that ooze toward the toe of the Great Ledge.
Meanwhile the vestiges of mainland life
crept eastward as the ice-cap shrank away,
surviving struggles on the higher ground,
but stopped here, where the ocean barred the path.

Thus, at the edge of ordinary forest
this Ledge became a marker for the place
where we, outcasts of Europe, landed slaves,
sugar, rum, the books of the ghostly creed
whose cruelties we turned upon the natives
in order to make sure of mastering—
with force and guile, theology and law—
the continent they pervaded from the West
behind the glacier and the buffalo,
only to find a boat-borne paler tribe
intent to fill their land with our begetting.
It's done. The nation's paved from east to west.
Its poisons drain from every last direction
past the Great Ledge into the whickering sea.

I wander through the grove beneath the Ledge:
hearts on the beech-trees stand at just the height
where lovers carve who are not fully grown.
A child's plastic toy, a coffee-pot
mark trivial and temporary campgrounds.
Woodpiles, a heap of ax-chips, of sawdust,
a pair of pine planks laid across the brook,
show that we're here, still living off the land.
Even the meadow wanted to be cleared
and kept that way, but not enough to win:
no one's taken the trouble to cultivate it.
The field has kept itself, in case of need,
for the exclusive uses of the Ledge,
whatever they may be. The Ledge needs nothing.
Standing behind the trees, above the water,
the ocean slowly pulsing down below,
the Ledge is where this continent began—
where, once we have passed by, leaving it barren,
the sea will inch up, overwhelm the Ledge,
to change the world and tell another story.

YE HAVE YOUR CLOSES

As grey damp covers this supine July
the mourning dove reiterates her moaning
through endless post-coital afternoons.
These days more lungs take ordinary air,
drain out its oxygen, and mingle it with carbon
than ever. Humans are breathing harder
than ever before in breathless history.

We have taught our children too much about comfort:
warm air, cool drink, hot sound, high speed, ripping
the planet inside out, clawing for carbon
to feed the ravening engines of convenience,
charming fossils out of the ground
to relinquish gases life inhaled from air,
cashing in the earth's bank balance of death.

We have taught our children too much about profit:
they have taken to burning bodies still alive,
forests that have furred the world's broad flank.
If dark and thickness close upon our lungs
and force us back to living under thatch,
on poles, in mists, by fever-blistered seas,
we'll mourn like doves, repeating as we grieve
how carbon kept us whole—and though the whole
world turn to coal, then chiefly live.

KEEPING ACCOUNTS

The country inn by the Missouri River
       lost all it had (except a pair of chimneys)
to trees, the only guests that came to stay.

Some day, the elders swore, *we'll tell you true:*
       but they forgot. Their eyes rolled up, and swift
oblivion rinsed out their episodes.

Precious few remnants got recalled again,
       though the best fathers kept a strict account
of the past on slates as bright as though they'd scrubbed them.

Volunteer appletrees in sheltered swales
       stand now for what's forgotten. Walls of stone
no one has had the patience to pull down

tell where our great-grandfathers cleared the land
       before we learned to live by information
traded for someone else's information.

Such stories! Elders cheerfully recounted
       each stride of all those pilgrimages made
into new country: how they felled the trees.

Old leather dead-pans spitting at the store,
       grannies around the stove, spoke memories of
a time when cattle recognized their masters

and everyone could number every lineage,
       each harvest and hard frost, keeping accounts
by gnawing on the nourishment of stories.

GENERATIONS OF SWAN

(For Sarah Elizabeth Jane Davison)

Sex—the unseen governor
of mood in a baby's fingers,
conditions her gestures as gently
as form commands the swoop
in the neck of a swan,
though she carry her gender as coolly
as the diamond-blue eyes
and shivering senses that extend
her self beyond body.

In what chromosomal interchange
her contours were specified
no one knows; yet, endowed
by thousands of forebears,
only she, universal receiver,
carries no gene of her own
to command her heir-apparent self.

Long anticipating her body,
the clans will have nudged her
to transform baby into child,
child into gap-toothed girl,
girl into woman, every ancestor
implicit in every gesture,
each grief, each amazement—just

as in middle life she may fail
to recall (surviving perhaps
as a haggard bent-kneed crone,
perhaps as a thickened matron)

whether the touch of her mother's hands
fondling her infant body
had whatsoever to do
with the colors she would wear
or the way she chose to walk.

How could this tottering baby
who lurches across a carpet
to bestow on her grandfather's lap
the ultimate gift of a spoon
anticipate the flush of desire
that young men two decades hence
will feel bulge in their throats
at the grace of her deep breasts,
that ancestrally curved neck,
and the legendary blue eyes?

CONCENTRATION

Look at that goldenrod! Blue-green when I patrolled
a week ago, this week it nods in gold,
bright gold, and no one noticed it go by.

My old dog twists around to gnaw her thigh
and nab a flock of fleas. Too late. Pursued
by what cannot be grasped, our thought can find
no path to light except through interludes
of darkness. Where's the center of the mind?

Think of my dark-haired architect upstairs,
whose buildings, stretched to measure for her clients,
somehow disarm all structural defiance
by taking place in shapes completely hers.
When vision grasps a volume to enclose
within a granite skin, its eyes impose
a set of shapes (in fact as in illusion)
by mixing space with time. Doors by exclusion
admit events. The window's glassy face,
abstracting light from heat, defines a space.

To saturate an emptiness in time
the access may be trivial as rhyme
to chalk faint boundaries for the unheard
and seal attention in a single word.
So Polyphemus' vision—as he groped his burred
and greasy sheep and willed his hands to bind
Nobody, the man who gored him blind
while his own animals were trotting past,
the favorite old ram the very last—
would harden in his skull, as was foretold,
helpless to reckon blue-and-green from gold.

TAKING PLEASURE

"Love? Nothing simpler," murmured the goddess—
and all my carefully husbanded breath
escaped me. Oh you may well imagine
the way things went, sprawling among cushions,
dozing away a dozen afternoons
thirsty for more kisses, a sweet lout
hitting the lottery on his first try,
scrawling the one poem that would make his name.

Each soul locks up its half-forgotten story
telling for instance how we worked our way
through twiggy thickets past crags of appetite
toward the one clearing where somebody will listen.

Which of us knows how you may "change your life,"
rip off the gloves of labor and breathe easy?
No way. With miles to run to get to the finish,
no one can balance accounts. The flowerbed's
unweeded, nothing in flower, either about-
to-bloom or just-gone-past-its-best. The dream
we pant for is the thought of a green shade
where someone else has finished up the chores
and the result is *us:*
a catch in the breath, the ripple of desire,
a mother's murmur to her favorite child.

After the faltering of ordinary daylight
the rainbow casts its colors, no one asking.

THE MOCKINGBIRD

Writing about you seems to tilt me into
a period posture. You were not an absolute
contemporary: your brilliance feathered you:
a bird of passage, flashes of mocking.
Perhaps I never got the hang of you
after more than two decades of your company,
but no one in ninety seasons gladdened me
more—such pleasure in spending mere time
in the same house with you, in different rooms.
You made me see as with two pairs of eyes,
two sensibilities: a Siamese life.

PEACHES

A mouthful of language to swallow:
stretches of beach, sweet clinches,
breaches in walls, pleached branches;
britches hauled over haunches;
hunched leeches, wrenched teachers.
What English can do: ransack
the warmth that chuckles beneath
fuzzed surfaces, smooth velvet
richness, plashy juices.
I beseech you, peach,
clench me into the sweetness
of your reaches.

EMERALD

How can we mourn for you,
having known nothing till
you chilled before our eyes
holding a fistful of hours?
While your breath crackled
and your skin grew grey
could we not have calmed
your shivering shoulders
or breathed back your heat?
You encountered
fresh air so rarely
after nine months as
carry-on baggage
that when your breath ceased
we too were left breathless.
Our words spent themselves,
like caresses, on your mother,
or in an arm draped over
your father's bowed shoulders,
or in a helpless handshake
for your parents' pale parents.

The child? Name? Oh yes,
the girl, I remember—who would,
I recall, have been christened
Emerald—put in so brief
an appearance that no one
thought to call for holy water,
and our grief had no time
to make headway, but stalled
motionless, leaving us
incurably angry, deprived
of anyone to blame
but our foolish selves, marooned
sailors, who had counted
on a long, cargo-crammed voyage.

THE PASSING OF THISTLE

This is our first summer without a dog.
Fifteen years of disgraces in the night
(tattered screen doors, overturned garbage pails,
unexpected puddles on the guestroom bed,
and other misbehaviors) have ended at last.
She had a way of posing in the landscape,
arranging herself against a screen of trees,
upon a lawn or on an outdoor deck
so as to bring out the hero in photographers
who could focus on the challenge of her darkness.
When on the move she carried less distinction:
a scottie, long in the barrel, short of leg,
she trotted country roads like city sidewalks,
so long as a glance behind her could confirm
the support of the authority that gave her hers.
Absent such authority, she panicked:
could be found, after a search, hysterically
galloping somewhere in the wrong direction
if we returned from shopping or the movies
through a region she had not known long enough to own.
On her home turf she brooked no trespassing,
at least by motorcycles, dogs, or horses,
though she'd roll over basely for human intruders.
The children who had grown up while she watched
were patient, watching her as age declined
from sleepiness to blindness, deafness and
incontinence. Before her last collapse
she lived her life entirely through the nose
and sense of touch. And as they watched her sleep
they saw their childhoods disappearing with her
and by so much ceased a little to be children.

I who had shared, in my two-legged way,
in what I could grasp of her doggy memories,
knew we had lived through all the same affections,
felt the same losses, searched through an empty house
for someone who would never be returning,
brooded on sights and voices that had vanished.

Perhaps she had a way of understanding
our loss that she could never share with me,
but now our past belongs to me alone,
now that she's gone, and no one else remembers
the weekends that we spent in the house together
letting each other in and out of doors.

CRACKS IN THE UNIVERSE

(For Qiu Deshu)

1. *Qiu Deshu*

Far from Shanghai and ill at ease among
the babble of gallery-goers, he caught the eye
of an American, swivelled his moon face
toward a wall of his paintings, asking anxiously,
"I see crack in universe. You see?"
Yes, I see. I see. He has soaked layers
of Chinese rice paper in inks as bright
as a severed artery gushing blood
or the wing of a little blue heron silvered with lightning
or a live chrysanthemum catching fire.
Beyond our sight-lines he has planted eyes
that catch the eyes of those who have eyes to see,
and lets the universe peer back at us.

2. *Valtellina*

Along this valley, doorsill of the Alps,
great River Adda slices through the mountains
due east due west. A festal summer sun
smiles at the northern slope as at a bosom
on whose round apron cataracts of grapes
bloom into crimson bubbles. River Adda's
southerly bank holds back a shadow forest
that shelters dark encampments of deer and boar.
The wine is called Inferno, juice of Hell.
After they've trampled it they gather mushrooms,
plants without leaves or sexuality,
attesting to the funerals of the trees,
the juice of hell, the phallus of the dead.

O Valtellina, guiltless as a crying
baby in the pathway of a flood,
may Hell protect you from utility,
damming or bottling you, sowing your banks
with spikes of utility towers, piercing your hills
with holes to bleed off arteries of steam
we humans may halter for our purposes:
feeding halogen highways, curling hair,
deranging sultry nights with a whirring fan.

3. *Beyond Sight Lines*

The wild remember what the dead retain.
Dogs bark and bristle at the noise of silence.
Shamans laid out portions of food for spirits
so that the gods would act on human need
in answer to a simple task, made pure
by emptying it of its utility.
Just so our prayers make tracks across a stream,
and reason can find no traces of a passage
although it knows the word has gone to ground.
Our lives have changed the earth, not merely scarred it:
it exhales intention as we pass.

4. *Edge*

Reason's hands reach out but cannot touch
the spectral evasions that have been ordained
but never pocketed. Call them immeasurable,
call them unknown, the limits of the mind.
We ride the world like monkeys on a stallion
we cannot curb or steer. Our names for it
insult the world: we'd strip its body bare
in appetite to govern. If we gained
control, we'd push ourselves to the abyss
that we have tried to think unthinkable.

5. *Waking*

At the far edge of sleep
or in uttermost despair
at the outcome of these dreams
we press beyond the boundaries
of ignorance and heartbreak.
"I see crack in universe. You see?"
O yes. I see. I see.

ABOUT TIME

(Musée d'Orsay, Paris)

Thousands who pass behind the great clock's dial
stop, stare through time across the city still
holding a Sacred Heart upon its hill.
The site exalts them, clicking snapshots, while
a dozen tongues exclaim at where they are:
above, and staring down the *Ville Lumière*
through time, told automatically. There:
the hands click forward, clocked beneath the *gare*.

A few steps past that view, they share a sight
that like the railroad will not pass again:
two eyes, myopic with eternal light,
conveyed their view to Now from vanished Then
a century ago: the blaze of day
lives in the timeless lilies of Monet.

MOTHER & CHILD #3

Nothing below the wrist? Hands are missing?
No way to thread a needle, grasp a hammer,
pluck strings, stir kettles, tease the drooping
curl of a lover's hair? Never a palm
against the cheek, never a pen between the fingers?
No hands, we finish second to the ape.

In the nightmare my mother's hands, lopped off,
left me helpless to be lifted up. A door
chillier than time would close between us,
thicker than the fact of her early death
over uneaten breakfast on her birthday.

Her face has faded, unfamiliar
as photos yellowing for fifty years.
Touch faded long since: "How can I keep in touch
when there is nothing to touch?" I asked myself.
Answer? Can't. No voice to recognize.
No face to smile at. No hands to lift me up.
Nothing's remembered but lips, the fleeting posture
of a woman crouching, the knot of a red bandanna,
the smell of a body powdered in the morning.

Time's accidents entrap and then release
the tiny puffs of memory that arrive
like signals sent in smoke from a distant tribe
whose messages we might have understood
if only we had spoken the right language.
All children learn the ways that breast and milk
and hands lift up the body of a baby.
Hands spoke the truth, and when they spoke we heard.

THE WAR OF THE PELICANS

Mocha pelicans peeled off above the lagoon,
its dark edge furred with borders of grey-green mangrove,
to feast before dark: flap, sail and stall, nose down,
then hurtle like javelins into the glossy water
with chest-crushing blows like mailed men bluntly jousting,
each time to emerge, to pause as though dazed, to toss
the beak like a censer and gulp down whatever luckless
pouch-ensnared mullet had witlessly caught the eye
and altered a cruising glide into *kamikaze*.
As daylight dwindled, the muster grew more ruthless.
The birds took targets to right and left in the dusk:
tiny fish who, blinded by sunset's angle,
fluttered in woe and death.
                              Alongside the mangroves,
silent as border guards, strode herons, white or blue,
to audit the big birds' clash. They kept their eyes
bent low above their business, or, sentry-like,
stole glances sidewise, alert for whatever peril
might change (behind and between the slimy roots
of the seemly mangrove, ancient shelter of herons)
a sanctuary into a weir where even the poorest
of fish would have acted the fool, in the dreadful clangor
of reddening light, to risk its earthly rest.

EVENING GROSBEAKS

tumble out of the air
chunk onto treelimb
awkward gold smudges
resolving into wedges of beak
pursued and supported
by a gang of blunt bullies
in black coats
a rouse of fellows
out on the town
sporting yellow visors
on each black cap
white velvet flaps
on each broadbottomed tail
do not linger
gone

LITERARY PORTRAITS

> *...that man of song*
> *whom the Muse cherished; by her gift he knew*
> *the good of life, and evil—*
> *for she who lent him sweetness made him blind.*
>
> ODYSSEY VIII

1. *Letter from the Poetry Editor*

I write you this because, to your surprise
perhaps, I have grazed through your poems
as a chance visitor to your room might, noting
a pair of green slippers dropped beside the bed
and a half-finished letter on the desk—
which I have read. From such clues I can guess
that you allowed yourself to be interrupted,
and why you walked outside, and where. I know
something about your habits, how you touch
the words you choose, which edges you have crimped,
those which you've not been able to unbalance.
I know more than you want me to, perhaps,
about what you are obsessed by, whether you
have ravished your desire or been flung back;
I've read the sayings that you call your own,
the ways you take to try to make them ours.

You might not think that you were spied upon,
but take my word, at least, that I was here
when you were out. And found you in, at home.

2. *Autobiographer*

He struck an attitude, head bowed
to show us all that he had mingled freely
but not enough to hold responsible
for much. He sketched some scenes: other men acted
while he stood still, helpless to avert
any event that might lead to regrettable outcomes.
He strained to get the tone of it just right,
confessing fears of climbing, fears of storm,
and his repeated lack of influence:
to write that down seemed to relieve his mind.
He had troubled the waters of his time
sufficiently to claim a rank above
anonymous, a notch below obscure,
a name that didn't count, such felonies
as made nobody mad. He chose his life
to sit well on the page, a shapely story
told well enough to publish, not to read.

3. *The Lost Notebook*

These poems do not live; it's a sad diagnosis.
SYLVIA PLATH

They might as well have stiffened in their sleep
as jilted this way, spilled like crumpled Kleenex
in a taxi's back seat. What disrespect.
Their phony starts and impotent conclusions
have caged them in for years, nosing unuseably
at the mesh of sense and never getting through.
Yet none of them had drowned in memory:
a few survivors crawled ashore somehow
into a typescript, and a few were rescued.

Who would have missed the notebook anyhow?
I couldn't quash a feeling of relief
as the one responsible—the guardian
of mishaps cleverly preserved from view.
Yet what if they revived, having been snuffed
like a deported family, soused in the death-pits,
who had bought black-market documents in Salt Lake City?

Those poems were worse than nuisances. They'd suck
my life out, limp on the shelf unfinished—
but now they're crisp, revived: the notebook's rescued,
and, Christ!, I'm back in charge, I who abused my trust
like the nanny who gassed the children and hopped a plane
for a hideout and a new identity
as English-language tutor in Brazil.

4. *The Heroine: A Sequel*

Your poet has lain immortal for twenty-five years
hissing in fury, radiating rage,
while you—doomed to outlive her, loathing her alive
as deeply as she did her demented self—
try her case now at the bar, finding her guilty.

All her hypocrisies, her jealousies,
those poor misdeeds for which she paid in full,
are reconciled in your implacable accounting:
you balance against her life (so achingly misspent)
the value of the goods she left behind her—
sorrow, orphans, love, undying fame—
while you, her loyal survivor, act as champion.

Claw out the eyes of every enemy.
Excoriate the heresies. Drive home
the points of her poems like nails. Make sure
your darkened version of the tale is told.
Defend her memory from mistaken praise.
Stand and slash at the world in her empty place
back to back with your dearest love, her shadow.

5. The Canoneers

*If a pig wandered up to you during
a bacon-judging contest, you would
say impatiently, "Go away, pig!
What do you know about bacon?"*
RANDALL JARRELL *in
"The Age of Criticism"*

Judgment sustains, as one of us once wrote,
*literature institutionally. It is
the crucial critical faculty in the
maintenance of a literary canon.*
That's how we got put into this position
of passing critical judgment on the poets.
You understand? We have a job to do.

Some artists help us in our work. Not poets.
We've tried it, asked the poets to explain
what some of their poems mean: yet their responses
hardly illuminate our understanding
of postmodernism, the creative process,
or of the deconstruction of their work.
In fact, they multiply tautologies.
I know they're short on systematic thinking,
but you'd expect a little *quid pro quo*
considering how much depends on us:
posterity can't hope without our help
to cite those poets worthy of the canon
or ferret out their failures and their runts,
those without names, the children of the egg.
So poets hate our guts. They know we know it.
Each time I hear them talk away the night
they leave me without anything to say.

Maybe I'd be one—if I had the time.

6. *In Memory of Robert Fitzgerald*

Suavis justorum fragrat odor tumulo
ST. VENANTIUS FORTUNATUS *

Any entering footgear drew a squeak
from the beeswaxed tiles in the skewed corridor
of the sixteenth-century convent employed
as a Springfield poet's refuge. Visible under
a ping-pong table across the hall from the chapel,
a set of golf clubs slumbered in their bag.

Each morning, on the *piano nobile*,
the poet construed a score of lines of Homer
in a double-doored room made precious for his purposes
next to the *sala* where massive cabinetry
and an untuned piano slept as in a fable.
The *autostrada* grumbled miles below
the parish of St. Fortunatus of the Hills.

The villa, refuge for his wordly work,
was skewing an ancient epic into perspective;
are saints not painted, shrined in cloaks of gilt,
in tribute to the odor of sanctity?
Some poets can transform one tongue into another
despite a rattle of talk fuming up from the kitchen
where village girls are cutting *fettucine*
before a fireplace vast enough to roast sheep.

And if at noon the poet abandons his meters
to shoulder his golf-bag, and his lithe wife drives him
to a nearby nine-hole sparsely-seeded course,
and with narrowed eyes each smites a small ball,
balanced between tufts, from hole to hole—
odor of chocolate drifts down on their contest
between the cypresses and oleanders
from a factory fuming in the mounded hills
unto which the golfers lift up their sad faces.

Though Saint Fortunatus was a noted glutton,
vexilla regis prodeunt;
and you, proud harper, translated your epitaph:
"You speak with art, but your intent is honest.
The Argive troubles, and your own troubles,
you told us as a poet would,
a man who knows the world."

7. *Shelved*

Pinched on a shelf between Dante
—or Edward Davison—
and Emily Dickinson,
these poems fret at their shelf-life,
always upstanding.
They yearn to sprawl into brain-life,
heart-life, loose as a starlet.
How to escape?

By acting as I wanted:
seize you with a flush
of passion or recognition
inciting you to lay hands on
this book. To look inside:
not into me, into you.

* "[The poems of St. Venantius Fortunatus] are little letters in verse, reminiscences
of dinners where the fish was as subtly flavoured as the Falernian, of churches where
the sunlight wavered on the ceiling as on sea-water, of the midday halt in a wood,
July heat and dust and the lapse of spring water and a tired man lying on the grass
and chanting Virgil to himself, or the Psalms . . . *Vexilla regis prodeunt* was written
for the coming of a fragment of the Holy Rood to Poitiers: five hundred years later
it was the marching song of the men who fought for the Holy Sepulchre."
                                           HELEN WADDELL, *Medieval Latin Lyrics.*

THE ORACLE: SAMPLE QUESTIONS, STOCK ANSWERS

Q: What is our country's fate?

O: *All this nation's foes agree*
That it's frightening to be free.

Q: Can things go on getting better? Are they really getting
worse?

O: *Raise your spirits, bold and plucky:*
The other end of wrong is lucky.

Q: Can things go on getting worse? Might they get better?

O: *If a rich man dream of fire,*
Let him wake to his desire.

Q: What can we do to help our children?

O: *Wish the single mother joy:*
Her baby might have been a boy.

Q: What is the matter with our children?

O: *Anorexic, roly-poly:*
Everything that lives is holy.

Q: How can we help our parents?

O: *Take whatever gift they give:*
Satisfaction helps them live.

Q: Has the world got a chance?

O: *Would you call it wrong or right*
That Last Day turns into First Night?

Q: Where, how, can we find peace?

O: *Let the donkey at the gate*
Take possession of your fate.

Q: Will anybody be left after we die?

O: *If nobody is there to see*
    You, what is the use of me?

Q: Can I escape my fate?

O: *Would it be your lucky day—*
    The only one to get away?

Q: Will our side win?

O: *All good people come to dust*
    As all evil people must.

Q: Will those people *ever* learn?

O: *In the homeland of the rat*
    Only profiteers grow fat.

Q: Is the world coming to an end?

O: *Torque and friction; twist and bend;*
    Earth is not the user's friend.

AT SIXTY

I have pried up, brushed off the self in me
that hugged secrets—the griever, the night walker,
the peeping-tom who promised to reform,
thumbing through porn all day. Acknowledge all
his lapses, his intensity. Never fault him for feeling:
fault him for what he endangered: creeping into
beds so sweet that he could not recall the breathing.
He bubbled promises to keep his lovers
deaf to the lofty inflections of a desire
that had no mind to remember what it had sworn,
or whom it had been sworn to, or when. Could he expect
to anticipate the lurches of his guilt?

Well, things have changed for the good. The world looks clear.
That self has bleached: his harshest needs are gone.
Yet sometimes at the drawing in of day
when I am too beaten down to lift a spoon
I taste the sharp pepper of his cruelty.

NOTES

p. 243: "one of the experts": Noel Perrin, author of *First Person Rural, Second Person Rural, Third Person Rural,* etc.

p. 245: "Lexington," "Hoppy," "Chipmunk": the farm animals were mostly named by children. The last line alludes to "The Circus Animals' Desertion" by W. B. Yeats.

p. 252: The title and the last line allude to George Herbert's "Virtue."

p. 256: The last lines allude to Book IX of *The Odyssey.*

p. 257: "L'amour est si simple." Arletty to Jean-Louis Barrault in *Les Enfants du Paradis* (a film by Marcel Carné and Jacques Prévert, 1944).

p. 260: Thistle, a scottish terrier, lived from 1973 to 1988.

p. 262: Qiu Deshu (1946–   ) spent 1985–1986 in residence at Tufts University, where he painted, among much other work, murals on commission for the student union building. When last heard from he had returned to his home in Shanghai, but his paintings have been exhibited worldwide.

p. 265: The Monet paintings on the top floor of the Musée d'Orsay in Paris (formerly the Gare d'Orsay) have never been more dazzlingly lit.

p. 267: Near Boquerón, Puerto Rico, January 1987.

p. 273: The quoted passage concerning "judgment" came from *The New York Review of Books* and owes its origins to Leo Bersani.

p. 275: Edward Davison (1898–1970), the author's father, wrote *Poems* (1920), *Second Poems* (1923, in *Poems by Four Authors*: J. R. Ackerley, A. Y. Campbell, Edward Davison, and Frank Kendon), *Harvest of Youth* (1926), *Some Modern Poets* (1928), *The Heart's Unreason* (1931), *The Ninth Witch* (1932) and *Collected Poems* (1940).

p. 276: "The Oracle" was drafted for Boston's "First Night" celebrations, December 31, 1988.

HARMONICS

(*1994*)

IN MEMORY OF NATALIE WEINER DAVISON

(1899–1959)

*No wonder there are those lights of suspicion moving
endlessly over memory and its faces
over the way of memory itself the way
of remembering which is the way of forgetting*

from "The View" *by* W. S. MERWIN

THE SILENT PIANO

Oh, how it sounded fifty years ago!
Schubert impromptus, the ripple of arpeggios,
poignant accompaniments to Schumann,
grounds to Campion, duos to Wolff.
Picked at before breakfast by children learning Czerny,
thundering under the fingers of visiting virtuosi,
it knew sound largely from the touch
of my mother's fingers, now thirty-five years dead.
Who of late has made its strings tremble?

I keep it tuned, try to find a musician
to touch it while I sing, but such skilled friends
have departed, and those here whom I love
cannot or will not play. So the Steinway
sits, polished, leashed, silent, positioned
in the salon, unable to make music,
shrunk into furniture. The making of music
dwindles into harmonics from the past.

ADAGIO IN G-MINOR
(*Molière* and Albinoni)

Bleeding, bleeding, while the music throbs
his life away, he's carried on men's shoulders
up an eternal flight of stairs. His ruffled
shirt drinks down his blood. His glittering eyes surrender
their light. When the blood stops, the light will.

The image of the dying playwright rips
my dreams each time a high, heartbroken cadence
evokes the name of a second-rate composer
who, for once in his life, stirred, awakened
the depths of art and roused his tinny talent,
opening his being to the tears of things.

THE ORDEAL TREE

Dark green spearheads
of leaves are poised
at the causeway's edges
between Clearwater and Tampa
to poison the grazer with
evergreen foliage
nourishing blossoms
of tropical pink
drifting like flotsam
along the highway's shoulders
among picnic fires
that char beef whose fat smoke
drifts downwind and blurs
the vision of brown pelicans
skimming at twilight across
the mirror of the great bay

In this soft climate
clumps of oleander
adopt the role of
cedar-of-the-southland
weed-trees that run interference
for habitations and housecats
familiar of palm fronds
fencing settlers in
fastening sand in the soil
casting leaves in the off-season
into gutters crammed with compost

The oleander teems unrelentingly
outlives importations
palms pines people that invade
from more troublesome climates
cousins of the oleander
dogbane in the meadow
vinca familiar
blue-flowered periwinkle
in the window-box

and other diversified
Apocynaceae
measure out their medicines
hemp ornaments
dreams unruly death

"I HARDLY DREAM OF ANYONE
WHO IS STILL ALIVE"

(For William Matthews)

"Yes, Father, I too by pleasant streams
Have wandered all night in the Land of Dreams,
But, though calm and warm the waters wide,
I could not get to the other side."
—BLAKE

Red Auerbach fumed into my sleep last night
at my late grandmother's Upper-West-Side apartment
along with John Berryman, each to argue the practise
of a delicate craft. John Paul II prepared pasta.
What a party! Night after night such visitations!
Execrable, some of them, betrayals that seem
centuries old. A shrink in a Land Rover,
pipe clenched in his teeth, glares out over
the heaped cadavers of a flock of sacrificed lambs;
a senator's sherry bottle tumbles out of his briefcase;
and, skittering from bush to bush, my father,
concealing filthied underwear behind his body,
stumbles his way to the shelter of the guest-house.

Shame, this is your sting, these are your victims;
and all the years of striving to forget
cannot erase the presence of the dead,
every wrinkled face of which is mine.

THE BLACK ASPEN

(For Robert Penn Warren)

"A good poet is someone who manages, in a lifetime of standing out in thunderstorms, to be struck by lightning five or six times; a dozen or two dozen times and he is great." —RANDALL JARRELL

On a road to the house of a dying friend—
    lacklustre journey—I halted the car
by the edge of a raging riverbend
    beneath domed mountains. I'd walked just far

enough for my blood to seep some sense
    into cramped legs and my steering arm,
when a pair of grouse thundered over a fence
    from their covert of ferns and struck alarm

in a doe, stock still in the road ahead,
    who tensed her loins for a bolt of leap
to rid herself of this dreadful biped
    striding her way like a ghost asleep.

So nature salvaged me again.
    I'd nearly lost track of my destination
when a thrush started carolling in the rain
    as though joining in on a celebration.

Signals appeared beside the stream
    between two aspens, pale in the wood:
the middle tree shone with no natural gleam.
    I saw it had charred alive where it stood.

Lightning had licked it halfway down,
    blackened its trunk, scorched its root,
leaving it green in shaft and crown
    with a rug of charcoal under its foot.

The river rumbled, the aspen swayed.
　　The forest thrush sang on, sang on
as I veered from the facts and hurried away
　　　to the house where a poet would soon be gone.

September 15, 1989

GREAT GRANDMOTHER

(For Frances Ray Truslow, 1908–1989)

No death is ever final. The morning paper
will keep on plopping on the dewy grass
each sunrise till someone notices that no one
has been traversing the lawn of late to fetch it.
The telephone will not be answered by
the voice I spoke to every Saturday.
The loving beloved body no longer holds
its softened shape. The feet that shuffled from
the garden to the house will never move
again. The dimpled arms will never embrace
her sweet descendants. Ordinary facts.

Less ordinary facts: a volunteer tree
took its chances shading her Florida porch
and seemed to borrow some courage from the woman
who kept a tribe alive while others died.
She wept her dead but gave strength to the living,
those who brought new spouses to her shore,
grandchildren and great-grandchildren. She endured,
through others, for herself. She showed her pride
in dedication to each renewal of life,
warming her precious eggs in one filigree nest,
settling above them, certain as the sunset
that these three chicks would multiply forever.

THE UNFROCKED GOVERNESS

(For Elizabeth Bishop)

Round of face, with dimpled chin and cheeks
framed by her plumage of white hair,
the poet took a cup of tea and spoke
in stolid, undemonstrative discourse
six inches short of gossip. She disdained
the routine poets' talk of poetry
and poets, what she read, what she disliked,
even the poetry that she adored.
Something beyond this flickered in her eyes,
a glint of mischief or irreverence,
neither disclosed to me, although much later
I read of passions, fury, suicide,
legendary benders lasting weeks. Ah, how
could this dear old lady, orphaned as a child
by madness, give hostage to it in
the loves she chose, the fellow-poets who,
loving her work and loving her, went mad
and died by striking at their enemies:
themselves? And she? Observant of gentility,
of the affections and obsessions, wrote
with painful effort, though the consequence
felt easy as the breath of summer. Pain
dogged her life, yet she insisted: *Write it!*

THE NARCISSISTS

O what self-love their kindness shows,
filling your glass before it has been emptied,
making their house your house. The pool?
Jump in. The boat? Go on, take a ride.
Dinnertime? A gift at every plate,
each one to remind you how loving your host can be,
how fortunate you are to be a guest.
Their comradeship speaks itself so warmly
that you lose your balance: this is not friendship,
not exactly: this is the way they teach
you to love them for themselves.

UNCOMPROMISING POSITIONS

(In Memory of N. B. B. J.)

Face to face, cross-legged on the floor,
a candle ablaze between them,
the lovers gnawed each other with their eyes.
Between these raptures and the harsh divorce
lay fourteen years and four cherished children.

He, trenchcoated foreign correspondent,
barely survived exposure to shot and shell;
she, after he wandered,
by now a grandmother,
earned her Doctorate in Blood Sacrifice,
marched in a hundred demonstrations,
instructed unendurable regions of the mind.

At her funeral speakers declared
their testimony to her unsettling effects:
laughter without humor, humor without laughter,
voracity of love, implacable I-Thou.

Her absence leaves us memory of the candle,
a sacrifice of light consuming itself
yet leaving us shadowed:
the self-erasure of flesh,
the immolation of self,
the leper's kiss.

THE PHILANDERER

No matter if she missed him,
while he was traveling
she never telephoned.
He called in at every stop:

from Atlanta
(where he'd toppled a tipsy
popsy in a pink dress),

from San Francisco
(where a generous odalisque
awaited him, naked
on purple paisley sheets,
her door unlocked),

from Denver (where an avid
angry divorcee flashed
her hysterectomy scar
in a barren motel),

from Los Angeles
(where a sloe-eyed expert
in seduction chauffeured him
simply to her Murphy bed),

and from errands in New York
(vast borrowed apartments)

or Washington
(government-expense hotels
resilient with rendez-vous).

Wherever he travelled
he telephoned
to tell her the truth:
that he loved her,
exceeding all others.

Yet she never lifted the phone
except to his ring,
carefully sparing them both
intractable questions:

could devotion survive
such steamy compulsions,
such furtive random releases?

AFTER THE EXORCISM

How could my shadow go missing?
  Callow, treacherous child,
were you misfiled?
  Might you have nabbed a new habitat,
grabbed a slow train at the fright station
  to steam, hiss, shudder out?

Gone, however. Your once-dreaded darkness is missed.
  I feel its absence like a cavern,
what's lost in outdated newspapers,
  slurred gossip at the tavern,
smudged traces of disembodied faces
  cutting capers, half-remembered
napes I may once have kissed.

Merciless sunrise stuns into flight such faces,
  bringing to light their features
in rout from the crisp world,
  a whickering garble of traces
from sterner reality, hallowed creatures
  with vision unfaded, speech unfouled.

O Shadow, decamped with all my nuances,
  exertions, constrictions, bleaching me white,
evidently but not quite
  empty, unrecollecting each
of the unfiled dimensions of time:

you leave me stalled, foundering,
  sleepless, beached on the grit
of this tone-deaf, brilliant, odorless instant.

JOURNEY TO THE INTERIOR

The medical machine
winks out its blue and green
over my patient-bed
and flickers at my head

while a physician plumbs
my inner pathway, drums
up fiber-optic chords
to light his forced march inwards.

The pressure of outside air
unmasks my passages there:
mauve, rose and mother-of-pearl,
pulsating and aswirl

in humid light! I stir
upon the monitor,
blesséd sight, to see
the very core of me.

Ignore the muted noise
of my private gastric voice:
this endoscopy traces
the silence of secret places,

where who could have suspected
such traffic, undetected
within the body's crêche
of this too solid flesh?

THE BREATH OF LIFE

I heard your key in the door. It swung in,
left you, swung back, shutting the world out flat.
Your handbag tumbled to the floor
as your arms reached out to me. Your scented body,
held up by the whiteness of the wall,
reeled with desire. I stumbled to you,
your garden district, where we gasped
and trembled together like fellow flowers.

You gave me breath of life in the liquor
of your kisses. For months you kept me breathing
through afternoons of love in all those cities.

We sighed so deep while stroking and swimming
in one another's mouths and willing bodies,
we nourished cells that had a mind to die.

Flies buzzed through those curtained rooms. We'd get up
from bed for mozzarella, tomatoes,
and sigh down and drown together in sleep,
dreaming of love and death and tranquil oceans.

MELONS

Breast-shaped, boat-shaped, ball-shaped, wrinkled, smooth,
coasting on compost, scrabbling over desert,
pale green, dark green, sandy, grooved or mottled,
melons engorge themselves on expensive water
drawn from dark by the pumping of leafy engines.

I've longtime dreams of melons, of desire,
reposing in them every humid sweetness
bursting with every exquisite sensation.
In youth, in orgy dreams, I'd smash the melon
with craggy cudgels. Or the ripened melon
would soften, warm itself with human ripeness,
inviting me to penetrate the center,
there to dissolve in an unearthly rapture.

Now, though, those treasures, disembodied, vanish
in geometric chill, hollowly harden,
remote as emeralds in imagination,
brightening a portion of the visible spectrum,
leaving me dry and seedless, toneless, blank,
a vine without a melon, without purpose,
no expectation, no reward, no melon.

DEATH IS THE MOTHER OF BEAUTY

Maples, my maples and cedars,
hickories, crabapples,
birches and black cherry:
don't expect immunity
from your humble custodian.

This is no climate
for immortality
to spring from the bodies
of fallen giants
that tumble and rot
across paths nobody uses.

Keep your places, trees!
Only someone like horny Orpheus
would urge that you trouble
to budge yourselves—and he
was long ago stricken
by an overdraft of grieving.

EQUINOX 1990

My dreams slip off like eels
leaving no trace of themselves
in the tepid fluids
of my body's self-sustaining.
Do not desert me, mother, sister, beloved,
do not fade into absence or sleep.
I yearn for a voice to hear,
an ear to hearken,
a hand that can feel my fingers
through the corona of our tingling.

I have displaced every grain of anger.
I can't shed a tear for a lost child.
My body feels as bland as milk.
Take me, memory, if you still love me,
take me wherever you will. I am as light
as a mummy, dry as papyrus.
For all I know I am as dead
as the already dead.

FROM THE OUTLAND

As autumn marched, the pond was drained
    that in summer bobbled a thousand mallards,
a quartet of swans, countless gulls, a tenacious
    trio of catfish-gobbling cormorants.

As winter approached, the water level lowered,
    scattering waterbirds, uncovering
the floor of the tarn, rubble-strewn
    with plastic cups, soggy leaflets, bottles,

only the last staunch rabble of mallards
    dabbling the ooze of the bottom. One lone duck,
white, fat, and foreign, flightless, had somehow
    been transported from farmyard or garden,

some child's pet, no longer convenient,
    remanded to the park in high season,
where, clumsily mimicking the swans, she drifted
    through dwindling daylight. The sun sets early.

She floats, then waddles, lonely and colorless,
    as the darkness and the cold clench in around,
        and then, at last, black Tuesday, disappears.

IN QUERCY, 1993

In woods beyond these walls
    of limestone dripping green
festoons of moss, bird-calls
    speak up for the unseen

thousands who, unarmed
    with crossbow, bayonet,
their stony fields once farmed
    with compost, mattock, sweat.

This ancient stony lane
    a herd of sheep impels
through conquered Aquitaine,
    obedient to bells.

Few humans ever walk
    here on the lonely *causse*,
past poppy on its stalk,
    alyssum, daisy, rose.

Malnourished by our past,
    we've travelled far to seek
in rusty, lime-encompassed
    upland, a mystique

that long ago unstrung
    the warfare and the reaping.
We're centuries too young
    and have been oversleeping.

MOTHER CHURCH

St. Mary's Cathedral, San Francisco
(For Belluschi, Nervi, Kepes, Lippold)

With four feet planted on four standpoints
and cocked so that a sacred heart
may lift the tonnage of her mighty roof,
she levers it toward an elemental crest—
sun-blaze, blood-blaze, leaf-blaze, sea-blaze—
and fuses these energies into a true cross
that sifts splinters of outdoor daylight
earthward through air toward an altar.

We kneel beneath a maze of honeycomb hexagons
as crazed as the salt plain where Lot's fool wife
turned her face homeward, salted herself away.

Inside Mary's eggshell a cloud of light
glitters a blessing at the core of worship.

Her tabernacle gently accepts its arts—
stone, words, light, music—
into the cradleweight of Mother Church,
tenderly hoisted by the hands of men.

> *You who enter this sanctuary,*
> *Whether to gaze or pray,*
> > *Take comfort from the mystery*
> > *Of enraptured artifice.*

NEW YOR I

New Yor I! Graveyard bristling with monuments
and receptions for business purposes!
Has my right hand lost its cunning?
It can't remember how to spell your name:
unless I scowl, my keyboard won't offer
the *K:* it throws up *I* instead.

I was actually born on your streets,
Lexington at 76th. So was my mother.
My parents were married there, and so was I, once.
My mother, father, mother's mother and father
spent much of their lives dying there.
Talk about roots? Better call me
New Yorker, *New Yor I*, on your distaff side.

A Boston wag once said, "If you're from New York,
you're Jewish; if you're not, you're not." Not bad.
My father, reared in Yorkshire, came to the
new city in hot pursuit of Natalie Weiner.
Reader, she married him. I drop the *K* and write
an *I* instead: What am I asking with my *I*s?

Walking along West 12th Street, I had to cower
by the brownstone wall while two men
at the sidewalk's core, grunting and snarling,
scooped with drawn switchblades at one another's vitals.
We passers-by waited till we dared pass.
Many of my friends, when New York lurched,
jumped, it seems. When they have things to make
they find a place in the country and force their bloom.
If they have great need for money, they
hunker in town, behind the locked doors
of penthouses and limos, lounge at marble desks,
barking and whining into telephones
whose trade mark reads *Patrician*,
tapping instructions, quicker than brain-speed,
demanding quicker responses

from anyone unluckily out to lunch
or anyone fatally out of town.

Decades ago, on a holiday morning, a black girl
knocked at my apartment door and gave herself
to me for a glass of water. A white friend
took me to a darkened bar, where trade
postured and preened, wary between mirror walls.
Sex had something to do with it.
Along my dream-streets women beckoned me,
their breasts bared, faces insistent,
eyes aglitter with a brightness
that I could not imagine satisfying.
Epiphany: a conclave, gin-and-tonic,
at which the hostess sat down in the chicken mousse
before serving it. She burst into tears,
locked herself, glass in hand, into the bathroom
and emerged an hour later, engaged to be married
to a near-stranger. Sex had something to do with it.

New Yor I, city of clusterers, gravedigger
of friendship, Babylon's standard-bearer,
how can I capture the smirk on your face?
I cringe at the walls of your museums and theatres,
wriggle into your soft beds, sink in your restaurants,
Mighty Manhatta! while I cower at your bullies,
your parochial arrogance, your firestorms of gossip,
your snickering put-downs of out-of-towners.
I had better renounce you, *Newyori*,
risk dismissing my name (common property)
and my inheritance by trashing my birthplace.
Why not? My heart has left town.
Sleek in your worsteds and leathers,
you yearn westward toward the India
you have yet to take passage for.

OUR EYES: A FAMILY GALLERY

This is the room my life's recorded in:
its archives are stacked in notebooks on shelves behind me.
Its poetry surrounds me on three sides.
At the left end of the north wall: handsome and glowering,
my father's photograph, 1926,
(hair in glossy waves, dark-browed eyes
askance to his left in three-quarter face)
shows sadness and darkness preparing for rain.
Next to him, half remembered, hangs
a portrait of my mother as a girl,
her right eye wider than her left,
both brimming with tears.

Above them on the wall a charged scene:
I sit in short pants and white socks
on a stone bench before a hacienda-house,
next to the great poet.
At his left my mother, hair in a bun,
hands folded attentively in her lap,
wears her white coat open
to Christmas sunshine with an air of pride
at her propinquity to Frost,
who, sitting with eyes closed against the sun,
was younger then than I am, writing now.
On her left hand, my father sits, his left
arm thrown around my standing sister
who, at the age of four, hugs to her chest
a huge sunbonneted doll and squints into
the sun like all of us. That dazzled picture
has hovered over me for sixty years.

Above and to the right, floating in heaven,
Pickersgill's head of disembodied Wordsworth
hangs above my daughter's first good photo
showing a tidal pool, and, behind, a carpet of marshgrass
extending beyond the pool to a distant cedar.
At the waterside, necks extended like cannon,
three white geese are sounding their trumpets

("Let the harsh gabble and upbraiding cease")
to guard the wild marsh against encroachment
while, drawn up to their rear, a single duck
waddles, bewildered but noiseless.
                              They may be cackling at
an earlier portrait of Robert Frost at fifty,
formal in dark suit, white shirt, his eyes directed
(beneath a ceremonial mask from Mexico)
upon the musing portrait of my dead wife Jane,
who trades with Frost a glance as warm and shrewd
as he gives her. Those glances took them half
a century to exchange.
                              Next, now in color,
our son sits, chin in hand, brows knitted over
a puzzle on a table, while his daughter Sarah
laughs into the camera. Joan looks down
at her with love. Those pairs of sparkling eyes,
three-generational, rove in three dimensions.
Light from the marshland streams into the window
behind my handsome son's fine head, Achaian crest.

Westward, to the right, taking to the air,
an osprey lifts off from the branch of a Florida pine
into a sky of blue with puffy clouds
that hold no threat of rain: the raptor's wings
feather the air in strokes of rising power.
Only the camerawoman knows that the bird rose up
beyond the house of my first wife's mother
as though his spirit lifted with her death.

Last on this southern wall, in black and white,
a lone black Labrador retriever stands
at the foot of a narrow pier, anxiously peering
out across the salt marsh at flood-tide
so high, the dog can recognize no land
nor landmarks, scent-marks, houses nor cedar trees.
His whole wide world has been wiped out by water.

Beneath him, a square clock in black and white;
its hour and minute hands are painted red.

Barometer, hygrometer, thermometer
speak out their news in green. The time is seven
minutes short of 3:00. Humidity stands exactly
50-50. The heat is 70 Fahrenheit. The air
will hold up 30 inches in a glass.

Around the corner, facing my young father
across this rustling room, see old Walt Whitman
lithographed by Boardman Robinson, 1940,
gazing with intolerable benevolence
at the crowded population of the place,
regarding them, benevolent and dejected,
and at me, no picture, scowling in my deep brown chair
where I have spent hundreds of hours, like this one,
mixing the fixatives of an unfixed life.

UNDER THE ROOF OF MEMORY

(In Memory of Jane Davison)

1. *Pleas*

Please help us keep your memory alive.
When I leaf through what's left of you, stacked up
into a formless pile of crumbling paper,
my hand turns pages, and occasions blur
until I stoop for a mishandled pill
and cannot straighten up. Or yawn. Then
a whiff of the heat lightning of desire
flickers at the fragrance of a caress
forty years old, a darkened room in Kansas.
Who shall deliver me from the body of this death?

2. *Celebration*

You floated weightlessly above your body,
in utterances aerating anything
that crept within your reach. You loved releasing
the preposterous, always managing to fold it
into a phrase, as when you located *Star Wars*
as taking place in "the Marseilles of the galaxy."
Dwindling through the waning days of life,
you wrote in your last letter, "Simplify,
simplify seems to be the method to deal
with the uncertainties of my health, as we
apply rational faculties to solve problems
we never really thought of as problems: who
carries the dirty laundry down to the machine
in the basement, and who carries it up."
Setting your house in order. Simplifying it
into a church as your body prepared to die.

3. *Remonstrance*

Why can't you take your rest? You have been dead
so long that every cell of you has entered

310

my helplessly surviving body, leaching down
beneath the landscape to our children,
to the dear actuality of my second wife.
You could, like her first husband, live with us
as an invisible, cherished, and welcome presence.
You would be past sixty now. You would have stiffened,
whitened, would feel aches of your own,
and shuffle, smiling at your own decline
and other such absurdities: my own.

4. *Critique*

Is it worth much, this sedulous retelling
of the careworn beads of the body? Why must I
catalogue its youthful urges, its middle-aged
infelicities, its eldering need to finger
its entrances, dark witnesses to history?
Get shut of the obsessive self-regard
of the child, that temperature chart more passionate
in the terms of description than in the thing described!
What price forgetfulness? What price peace?

5. *Envoi*

Late in my life, I dream of us together,
clothed in the house whose peaked, protective roof
floats without burden over spacious rooms,
commodious, airy, bright as a church. Its walls
and roof, pulled out of touch by the intervention of time,
hold up a screen for love, a sleight of words.
We longed to keep a ravenous world at bay
by gazing down its glare and speaking well.

A NOTE ABOUT THE AUTHOR

Peter Davison was born in New York City in 1928, son of the English poet Edward Davison, who had emigrated to the United States a few years earlier, and who had a long career as a teacher, initially at the University of Colorado at Boulder, where Peter Davison was raised. He served at sixteen as a page in the U.S. Senate, and subsequently attended Harvard University and Cambridge in England. He became an editor at Harcourt, Brace at the age of twenty-two, moving to Boston in 1955 to work at Harvard University Press and then at Atlantic Monthly Press, where he remained for the next twenty-nine years, latterly as its editor-in-chief and director. His career as a poet began in 1963 when his first book, *The Breaking of the Day*, was chosen as the Yale Series of Younger Poets volume for that year. Since then he has published nine other books of poems. He is also the author of an autobiographical volume, *Half Remembered: A Personal History*, a work of biographical criticism, *The Fading Smile: Poets in Boston, 1955–1960*, and a book of essays, *One of the Dangerous Trades: Essays on the Work and Workings of Poetry*. In 1985 he severed connections with Atlantic Monthly Press (although he remains poetry editor of the magazine) and joined Houghton Mifflin with his own imprint.

A NOTE ON THE TYPE

The text of this book has been set on the Linotype in a typeface called Baskerville. It is a facsimile reproduction of types cast from molds made for John Baskerville (1706–1775) from his designs. The punches for the revised Linotype Baskerville were cut under the supervision of the English printer George W. Jones. John Baskerville's original face was one of the forerunners of the type-style known as "modern face" to printers: a "modern" of the period A.D. 1800.

Composition by Heritage Printers,
Charlotte, North Carolina
Printed and bound by Quebecor Printing,
Fairfield, Pennsylvania
Designed by Harry Ford